Bible Stories and Prayers for Teens With Deeper Meaning:

Inspiring Lessons on Faith, Courage, and Character Every Christian Teenager Should Know

Tobias Wright

Copyright © 2025 – Tobias Wright - All rights reserved.

No part of this book may be reproduced, distributed, or transmitted in any form or by any means, including photocopying, recording, or other electronic or mechanical methods, without the prior written permission of the publisher, except in the case of brief quotations used in critical reviews and other noncommercial uses permitted by copyright law.

This publication is intended for educational and inspirational purposes only. The stories, reflections, prayers, and activities included are based on biblical texts and traditional Christian teachings. While every effort has been made to ensure accuracy, this book is not intended to replace the Bible, professional counseling, or pastoral guidance.

Parents and guardians are encouraged to read and discuss these stories together with teens to provide guidance and support.

All Scripture quotations, unless otherwise indicated, are taken from the public domain version of the Bible.

Table of Contents

About Me 6

Creation and God's Purpose 7

Noah and the Ark 8

Abraham's Call 9

Joseph's Dreams and Trials 10

Moses and the Burning Bush 11

Crossing the Red Sea 12

The Ten Commandments 13

Joshua and the Walls of Jericho 14

Samson's Strength and Weakness 15

Ruth's Loyalty 16

Samuel Hears God's Voice 17

David and Goliath 18

David and Jonathan's Friendship 19

Elijah on Mount Carmel 20

Elijah Hears God in a Whisper 21

Esther's Courage 22

Job's Perseverance 23

Daniel in the Lions' Den 24

Shadrach, Meshach, and Abednego in the Fiery Furnace 25

Jonah and the Great Fish 26

The Call of Isaiah 27

The Valley of Dry Bones 28

The Birth of Jesus 29

The Boy Jesus in the Temple 30

The Baptism of Jesus 31

The Temptation of Jesus 32

The Calling of the First Disciples 33

The Sermon on the Mount 34

Jesus Calms the Storm 35

The Feeding of the 5,000 36

Jesus Walks on Water 37

The Good Samaritan 38

The Prodigal Son 39

The Rich Young Ruler 40

Zacchaeus the Tax Collector	41
The Last Supper	42
Jesus Prays in Gethsemane	43
Peter Denies Jesus	44
The Crucifixion of Jesus	45
The Resurrection of Jesus	46
The Great Commission	47
The Coming of the Holy Spirit	48
Peter Heals the Beggar	49
Stephen the First Martyr	50
Saul's Conversion	51
Peter and Cornelius	52
Paul and Silas in Prison	53
Paul's Shipwreck	54
The Armor of God	55
The Fruit of the Spirit	56
The Greatest Commandment	57
The Widow's Offering	58
The Parable of the Talents	59
The Parable of the Lost Sheep	60
The Parable of the Sower	61
The Parable of the Mustard Seed	62
The Parable of the Wise and Foolish Builders	63
The Parable of the Unforgiving Servant	64
The Parable of the Ten Virgins	65
The Parable of the Sheep and the Goats	66
The Road to Emmaus	67
The Ascension of Jesus	68
Philip and the Ethiopian	69
Ananias and Sapphira	70
Barnabas the Encourager	71
Paul Preaches in Athens	72
Paul Writes to the Philippians	73
Paul's Teaching on Love	74
Paul's Race of Faith	75
John's Vision of Heaven	76
Cain and Abel	77
The Tower of Babel	78

Jacob and Esau	79
Joseph Forgives His Brothers	80
The Call of Gideon	81
Deborah the Judge	82
Hannah's Prayer	83
Solomon's Wisdom	84
Nehemiah Rebuilds the Wall	85
The Fiery Furnace	86
Daniel Interprets the King's Dream	87
Daniel's Integrity	88
Jonah's Mission to Nineveh	89
The Faith of Job	90
The Faith of Abraham	91
Isaac and Rebekah	92
The Birth of Samuel	93
Elisha and the Widow's Oil	94
Elisha Heals Naaman	95
The Call of Jeremiah	96
The Call of Moses	97
The Bronze Serpent	98
The Walls of Jericho	99
The Song of Mary	100
The Shepherds Visit Jesus	101
The Magi Visit Jesus	102
The Boy with Five Loaves and Two Fish	103
Jesus Raises Lazarus	104
The Road to Damascus	105
The New Heaven and New Earth	106
Share Your Experience	107

About Me

My name is Tobias Wright, and I am honored to share these pages with you. From the earliest days of my life, I have been fascinated by the stories of the Bible and the way they connect to the struggles and victories of everyday life. I have seen firsthand how Scripture has the power to shape character, strengthen faith, and guide people through the most difficult seasons. Writing this book has been both a privilege and a responsibility, because my greatest desire is to pass on the hope and wisdom that I have found in God's Word.

I never set out to become an author in the traditional sense. My journey began with small conversations, journal entries, and devotionals written for young people in my church community. Over time I realized that the questions, fears, and challenges teenagers face are often the same ones that men and women in the Bible experienced long ago. The settings may be different, but the heart of the struggle is the same. In that realization I felt called to create something that could bridge the gap between ancient truth and modern life.

This book is the result of many hours of prayer, study, and reflection. I wanted to present the Bible not as a distant collection of old stories but as a living testimony that speaks directly into the hearts of today's youth. Each chapter is designed to encourage readers to see themselves in the experiences of biblical men and women and to find strength in the God who guided them. I believe that when young people encounter these stories with open hearts, they will discover that God's Word is not only relevant but also deeply personal.

My hope is that these stories will do more than inform. I pray they will inspire courage, shape values, and create space for reflection. I also hope they will spark conversations between teens and parents, friends, and mentors. Faith is not meant to be lived in isolation but in community, and I believe that when we share our thoughts and questions together, we grow stronger.

Thank you for trusting me to walk alongside you in this journey through the Bible. I am grateful for the opportunity to write and even more grateful that you have chosen to read. May these stories remind you of God's presence in your life, encourage you in moments of doubt, and lead you closer to the love of Christ.

With gratitude,
Tobias.

Creation and God's Purpose

In the very beginning, there was nothing but darkness. Then God spoke, and everything began to take shape. With His words, light pierced the darkness, separating day from night. He formed the sky, the land, and the seas. The earth came alive with plants, flowers, and trees of every kind. The stars, sun, and moon were placed in the heavens to mark time and seasons. The oceans filled with fish, the skies with birds, and the land with animals of all shapes and sizes.

But God wasn't finished. His most important creation was still to come. With great care, He formed the first man, Adam, from the dust of the ground and breathed life into him. Later, God created Eve so Adam would not be alone. Together, they were given the responsibility to care for the beautiful garden of Eden and rule over the rest of creation. Unlike everything else, Adam and Eve were created in God's image. That meant they reflected His character and carried a special purpose.

God looked at all that He had made and declared it very good. The world was full of beauty, order, and peace. There was no pain, no fear, and no brokenness. Adam and Eve walked in perfect relationship with God, enjoying His presence every day.

This story reminds us that every person, including you, was created intentionally by God. You are not an accident or a mistake. Just as Adam and Eve were given a purpose, you also have a role to play in God's world. Being made in His image means you carry value that nothing can take away. It also means that the way you live, speak, and treat others should reflect the One who made you.

When you look at the beauty of creation—the sky, the trees, the ocean—you see a glimpse of God's creativity and love. But His greatest masterpiece is people. That includes you. Knowing that truth changes the way we see ourselves and the way we see others. Everyone around you is also made in the image of God and is worthy of respect, kindness, and love.

- Prayer: Lord, help me see my worth as Your creation and treat others as valuable too.
- Reflecting Question: What does it mean to you personally that you are made in God's image?
- Key Verse: "So God created mankind in his own image, in the image of God he created them; male and female he created them." (Genesis 1:27)
- Faith in Action: Treat someone with kindness this week as a reminder that they are God's creation.
- Gratitude Prompt: Name three things in creation you are thankful for today.

Noah and the Ark

Noah lived in a world that had turned its back on God. Violence, corruption, and selfishness filled the earth, and people laughed at the thought of living in obedience to the Lord. Yet in the middle of all that darkness, Noah stood out. He wasn't perfect, but his heart was faithful. He walked with God when no one else cared to.

One day God spoke to Noah with a command that seemed impossible: build a massive ark because a great flood was coming. The ark would be a giant boat, long enough to carry Noah's family and pairs of every kind of animal. Imagine how strange this must have sounded. Rain had never fallen like that before. The idea of a worldwide flood seemed ridiculous. And yet, Noah listened.

Day after day he gathered wood, hammered nails, and explained to his neighbors why he was doing something so unusual. People mocked him. Some likely shook their heads, others laughed, and some may have whispered that Noah had gone crazy. Still, he kept building. His obedience wasn't about pleasing people but about trusting the God who had spoken.

When the ark was finished, the animals came just as God had promised. Two by two they entered the giant vessel, and Noah's family followed. Then the skies opened. Rain poured down, the earth shook, and waters rose higher than the tallest trees. The people who had laughed at Noah realized too late that he had spoken the truth. Inside the ark, Noah and his family were safe. The storm raged outside for forty days and nights, but God's promise held firm. Eventually the waters began to recede. When the ark finally came to rest on the mountains of Ararat, Noah opened the door to a new world. The ground was fresh, the air was clean, and the earth was ready for a new beginning.

As Noah stepped out, his first act was not to build a home or claim land but to build an altar. He gave thanks to God, recognizing that every moment of safety and every breath of life had come from Him. In response, God set a rainbow in the sky, a symbol of His promise never again to destroy the earth with a flood. Noah's story reminds us that obedience to God sometimes means standing alone. It shows that faith often requires trust when others think you are foolish. And it teaches us that God always keeps His promises.

- Prayer: Lord, give me courage to follow You even when others do not understand.
- Reflecting Question: Have you ever felt alone in doing the right thing?
- Key Verse: "Noah did everything just as God commanded him." (Genesis 6:22)
- Faith in Action: Choose one small habit to practice faithfulness this week.
- Gratitude Prompt: Write down one way God has protected you or your family.

Abraham's Call

Abraham was living in Haran, surrounded by family, comfort, and familiarity. His life was stable, and everything seemed predictable. Then one day, God spoke directly to him with a command that would change his future forever: "Go from your country, your people and your father's household to the land I will show you." God didn't say exactly where Abraham would end up. There was no detailed map, no list of guarantees, only a promise that He would guide Abraham step by step.

Imagine the tension Abraham must have felt. Leaving everything he knew meant walking away from the security of home, his relatives, and the culture he understood. At seventy-five years old, starting over in an unknown land was no small decision. Yet Abraham's trust in God outweighed his fears. Scripture tells us that "Abraham went, as the Lord had told him." He chose obedience even though he had more questions than answers.

God's promise was extraordinary. He told Abraham that He would make him into a great nation, bless him, and make his name great. Through Abraham, all families on earth would one day be blessed. Abraham couldn't have known that this promise pointed forward to Jesus, who would come from his family line to bring salvation to the world. What Abraham did know was that God was trustworthy, and that was enough to take the first step. So Abraham packed up his belongings, gathered his wife Sarah, his nephew Lot, and all their possessions, and set out for a future that only God could see. Each mile of the journey was a test of faith. Every step away from home was a step toward God's promise.

This story still speaks powerfully to us today. Sometimes God calls us out of our comfort zones into places that feel uncertain. It could be starting at a new school, moving to a new city, or making a difficult choice that others don't understand. Like Abraham, we may not have all the answers. But God doesn't ask us to see the whole picture. He asks us to trust Him for the next step. Faith isn't about having everything figured out. It's about believing that God knows the way even when we don't. Abraham's obedience reminds us that walking with God often begins with a single step of trust, even when the road ahead is unclear.

- Prayer: Lord, help me trust Your plans when I don't see the full picture.
- Reflecting Question: When have you had to step into something new and uncertain?
- Key Verse: "Go from your country, your people and your father's household to the land I will show you." (Genesis 12:1)
- Faith in Action: Try one new positive action this week trusting God is with you.
- Gratitude Prompt: List two blessings you've experienced after a change in your life.

Joseph's Dreams and Trials

Joseph was the favored son of Jacob, born to him in his old age. His father gave him a richly decorated coat, a gift that made his brothers jealous. They already resented Joseph because of the dreams he shared. In one dream, his brothers' sheaves of grain bowed down to his. In another, the sun, moon, and eleven stars bowed before him. To his brothers, these dreams sounded arrogant and insulting.

One day Jacob sent Joseph to check on his brothers as they tended the flocks near Shechem. When they saw him coming, their jealousy boiled over. "Here comes the dreamer," they muttered. Some wanted to kill him, but Reuben, the eldest, convinced them to throw him into a pit instead. Later, when a caravan of traders passed by, Judah suggested selling Joseph as a slave. They pulled him out of the pit and sold him for twenty pieces of silver. The brothers dipped Joseph's coat in goat's blood and showed it to their father, who believed his beloved son had been killed by a wild animal.

Joseph was taken to Egypt and sold to Potiphar, an official of Pharaoh. Even in a foreign land, Joseph worked faithfully, and God's favor was with him. Potiphar trusted him with everything in his house. But Potiphar's wife lied about Joseph, accusing him of trying to harm her, and he was thrown into prison.

Though innocent, Joseph did not lose hope. In prison he interpreted the dreams of Pharaoh's cupbearer and baker. His gift was remembered two years later when Pharaoh himself had troubling dreams. Brought before the king, Joseph explained the dreams, predicting seven years of abundance followed by seven years of famine. Impressed by his wisdom, Pharaoh made Joseph second in command over all Egypt.

When famine spread across the land, Joseph's brothers traveled to Egypt to buy food. They bowed before the governor, not realizing it was Joseph, and his childhood dreams came true. After testing their hearts, Joseph revealed his identity. The brothers feared revenge, but Joseph spoke with grace: "You meant evil against me, but God meant it for good, to save many lives."

Joseph forgave them and provided for his entire family in Egypt. What began as betrayal ended in reconciliation, and God's plan was fulfilled through Joseph's faith and endurance.

- Prayer: Lord, help me forgive and trust Your plan even when life feels unfair.
- Reflecting Question: How do you usually respond when someone hurts you?
- Key Verse: "You meant evil against me, but God meant it for good." (Genesis 50:20)
- Faith in Action: Choose to forgive one small offense this week.
- Gratitude Prompt: Recall one difficult time that later brought unexpected good.

Moses and the Burning Bush

Moses had fled Egypt years earlier and was living a quiet life as a shepherd in the land of Midian. Every day he guided the sheep of his father-in-law Jethro through the wilderness, searching for water and grass. It was a life of solitude, far removed from the palace halls where he had once grown up as the adopted son of Pharaoh's daughter. Moses had likely come to believe that his chance to do something great had already passed.

One day, while leading the flock to the far side of the desert, Moses came to Horeb, the mountain of God. There, something unusual caught his eye. A bush was on fire, but it was not burning up. The flames danced brightly, yet the branches and leaves remained untouched. Intrigued, Moses stepped closer to see this strange sight.

As he approached, a voice called out from within the fire, "Moses, Moses!" Trembling, he answered, "Here I am." The voice continued, "Do not come any closer. Take off your sandals, for the place where you are standing is holy ground." Moses obeyed, removing his sandals as his heart pounded with awe.

The voice declared, "I am the God of your father, the God of Abraham, the God of Isaac, and the God of Jacob." At these words, Moses hid his face, afraid to look at God. The Lord then said, "I have seen the misery of my people in Egypt. I have heard their cries. I am sending you to Pharaoh to bring my people out of Egypt."

Moses was stunned. He had fled Egypt as a fugitive, and now God was sending him back to face Pharaoh himself. "Who am I, that I should go to Pharaoh and bring the Israelites out of Egypt?" he asked. God replied with words that carried both power and comfort: "I will be with you."

Still uncertain, Moses asked what he should say if the people questioned who had sent him. God answered, "Tell them, 'I AM has sent me to you.'" God revealed His holy name, assuring Moses that His power and presence would go before him.

Though Moses felt weak and unworthy, God had chosen him for this mission. What seemed impossible to Moses was possible because God Himself would guide him. From that moment on, the shepherd who once believed his life was finished was called to lead a nation to freedom.

- Prayer: Lord, remind me that You can use me even when I feel weak or unworthy.
- Reflecting Question: What excuses do you make when you doubt yourself?
- Key Verse: "I will be with you." (Exodus 3:12)
- Faith in Action: Encourage someone this week who feels unsure about themselves.
- Gratitude Prompt: Write one talent or gift God has given you.

Crossing the Red Sea

The Israelites stood at the edge of the Red Sea, trapped between the rushing waters and the thundering hoofbeats of Pharaoh's army. Panic spread through the people as they looked back and saw the Egyptians coming closer. Their hearts sank, and fear filled the air. Some cried out in despair, accusing Moses of leading them to certain death.

Moses stood firm. He raised his staff and spoke with confidence, reminding the people that the Lord would fight for them. His words calmed the trembling crowd, even as the roar of the chariots grew louder. God's presence, in the form of a pillar of cloud, moved between the Israelites and the Egyptians, shielding them from harm.

Then Moses lifted his staff over the waters. Suddenly, a strong east wind swept across the sea. All through the night the waters divided, rising up like walls on each side, and a dry path appeared down the middle. The Israelites stepped onto the seabed, wide-eyed, walking forward with the sea towering above them. Parents held their children close. Families clutched what little they carried. Step by step they crossed, protected by the mighty hand of God.

Behind them, Pharaoh's army charged into the passage, determined to capture them. Chariots rattled over the ground, soldiers shouted, and the sound of iron wheels echoed between the walls of water. Yet God was not finished. As the Egyptians pressed forward, their chariot wheels jammed and confusion spread among the ranks.

When the last Israelite stepped safely onto the far shore, God commanded Moses to raise his staff again. At once, the waters crashed back into place. The sea swallowed the chariots and soldiers. Pharaoh's mighty army was swept away, and not one survived.

Silence followed. Then the people erupted in shouts of joy. They had been cornered, helpless, but God had made a way where there was none. On the far shore of the Red Sea, they lifted their voices in praise. Moses and the people sang a song of victory, declaring that the Lord was their strength and salvation. What seemed impossible had become the greatest deliverance they had ever seen.

- Prayer: Lord, help me trust You when I feel trapped by problems. Remind me that You can make a way even when I see no escape.
- Reflecting Question: What "walls of water" in your life feel overwhelming right now?
- Key Verse: "The Lord will fight for you; you need only to be still." (Exodus 14:14)
- Faith in Action: When you feel stressed this week, pause to pray before reacting.
- Gratitude Prompt: Thank God for one situation where He gave you a way out.

The Ten Commandments

The people of Israel had seen the power of God in ways they would never forget. He had brought them out of Egypt with a mighty hand, parted the Red Sea, and led them through the wilderness with a pillar of cloud by day and fire by night. Now they camped at the foot of Mount Sinai, waiting to hear what the Lord would say to them.

The mountain was covered with smoke, for the Lord descended on it in fire. Thunder rolled across the sky, and flashes of lightning lit up the darkness. The sound of a trumpet grew louder and louder, and the people trembled as they stood at the base of the mountain. Moses climbed up into the thick cloud where God was. There, God gave him words that would guide His people for generations.

The Lord said, "I am the Lord your God, who brought you out of Egypt, out of the land of slavery. You shall have no other gods before me." These words were not just rules, but a covenant, showing the people how to live in a way that honored God and protected their community.

One by one, God gave the commandments. They were to worship Him alone and make no idols. They were to keep His name holy and remember the Sabbath day as a time of rest and worship. He told them to honor their father and mother, to value life by not murdering, to be faithful in marriage, to not steal, to not lie, and to not covet what belonged to others.

The people listened with fear and awe. These commands would shape their identity as God's chosen nation. They were not only rules about worship but also instructions on how to treat one another with respect and justice.

When the people heard the thunder and saw the lightning, they begged Moses to speak to them instead of hearing directly from God, for they were afraid. Moses told them not to be afraid, but to remember that God had come to test them so that the fear of Him would keep them from sinning.

These words written on stone tablets would remain a foundation for God's people. Through them, the Israelites would learn how to walk in obedience, to honor God with their whole hearts, and to live in harmony with one another.

- Prayer: Lord, help me respect Your commands and see them as a gift.
- Reflecting Question: How can rules actually bring freedom instead of restriction?
- Key Verse: "I am the Lord your God... You shall have no other gods before me." (Exodus 20:2–3)
- Faith in Action: Choose one commandment and focus on living it this week.
- Gratitude Prompt: Write 2 ways God's guidance has protected you.

Joshua and the Walls of Jericho

The people of Israel stood before the towering walls of Jericho. They had crossed the Jordan River by God's power, but now they faced a city that seemed impossible to conquer. Jericho's gates were shut tightly, and its soldiers watched from the walls. To the Israelites, the task looked overwhelming. Yet Joshua, their leader, remembered God's promise that He would give them the land.

One night, as Joshua was near Jericho, he looked up and saw a man standing before him with a drawn sword. Startled, Joshua asked if the man was for them or against them. The answer came with authority: "Neither, but as commander of the army of the Lord I have now come." Joshua fell facedown in reverence, realizing he was in the presence of one sent by God. The commander told him that the battle would not be won by swords or spears but by the power of the Lord.

The next day, Joshua shared God's unusual instructions with the people. For six days, they were to march once around the city in silence. Seven priests were to carry trumpets made from ram's horns in front of the ark of the covenant. On the seventh day, they were to march around the city seven times, and when the priests blew the trumpets, the people were to shout with all their might.

The people obeyed. On the first day, the priests carried the ark, the trumpets sounded softly, and the army marched silently around the walls. The citizens of Jericho peered down in confusion, mocking the strange parade. Still, the Israelites returned to camp without a word.

For six days, they repeated the same strange march. Doubt may have crept into some hearts, but Joshua urged them to trust God's plan. On the seventh day, the people rose early. They marched once, twice, three times, until they had circled the city seven times. Then the priests lifted their trumpets and blew a long blast. Joshua commanded, "Shout! For the Lord has given you the city!"

With a mighty cry, the people shouted. Suddenly, the massive walls of Jericho shook and collapsed to the ground. The soldiers of Israel rushed in, and the city was delivered into their hands just as God had promised. The victory was not by strength, weapons, or clever strategy. It was by faith and obedience to God's word. The people learned that when God leads, even the strongest walls cannot stand.

- Prayer: Lord, help me trust Your plans even when they seem unusual or difficult.
- Reflecting Question: When have you struggled to follow God's direction because it didn't make sense?
- Key Verse: "By faith the walls of Jericho fell." (Hebrews 11:30)
- Faith in Action: Obey God in one small area of your life this week, even if it feels challenging.
- Gratitude Prompt: Thank God for one time obedience brought blessing into your life.

Samson's Strength and Weakness

Long before Samson was born, an angel of the Lord told his parents that he would be set apart to serve God. He was to take a special vow and never cut his hair, for his strength would be a sign of God's Spirit at work in him. From the moment he grew, it was clear that Samson had extraordinary power. He tore apart a lion with his bare hands and struck down armies that outnumbered him. The people of Israel looked to him as a judge and a deliverer, and his fame spread across the land.

But Samson's heart was not always as strong as his arms. Though chosen by God, he often followed his own desires instead of God's commands. He sought the company of women who did not share his faith, and this led him into dangerous situations. The Philistines, Israel's enemies, feared Samson's strength and wanted to trap him.

One day Samson fell in love with a woman named Delilah. The Philistine rulers came to her in secret, offering her silver if she would discover the secret of Samson's strength. Delilah asked Samson again and again, and though he played tricks on her at first, her persistence wore him down. At last, he revealed the truth: his hair had never been cut, and that was the sign of his vow to God.

Delilah waited until Samson was asleep, and as he lay resting, his hair was cut off. When the Philistines rushed in, Samson awoke, but the Lord's strength had left him. They bound him in chains, blinded him, and threw him into prison. The mighty man who once struck fear into armies now ground grain like a slave.

Yet even in his failure, God was not finished with Samson. As his hair began to grow again, his heart turned back to the Lord. During a great festival, the Philistines brought Samson out to mock him. Standing between two great pillars, Samson prayed to God one final time. "Sovereign Lord, remember me. Please strengthen me just once more." With all his might he pushed, and the pillars collapsed. The temple fell, destroying the Philistine leaders and ending Samson's life, but also bringing victory to Israel. Samson's story is one of incredible power and tragic weakness, but also of God's mercy. Though he stumbled, his final act showed that God can still use the broken and the humbled for His purpose.

- Prayer: Lord, give me strength to honor You and avoid temptation.
- Reflecting Question: What "weak spot" in your life do you need God's help with?
- Key Verse: "Sovereign Lord, remember me. Please, God, strengthen me once more." (Judges 16:28)
- Faith in Action: Identify one temptation and plan a way to resist it this week.
- Gratitude Prompt: Write down a time when God gave you strength in weakness.

Ruth's Loyalty

Naomi, her husband, and their two sons had left Bethlehem during a famine and moved to Moab. Life was hard, and tragedy struck when Naomi's husband died. Her two sons later married Moabite women, Orpah and Ruth, but after about ten years both men also died. Naomi was left alone with her two daughters-in-law, heartbroken and unsure of what to do.

When Naomi heard that the Lord had provided food for His people in Bethlehem, she decided to return home. She urged Orpah and Ruth to stay in Moab, telling them they would have a better chance of remarrying among their own people. Orpah, though sad, kissed Naomi goodbye and stayed behind. Ruth, however, clung to Naomi with deep devotion.

Ruth spoke words that have echoed through generations: "Where you go I will go, and where you stay I will stay. Your people will be my people and your God my God." With that promise, Ruth committed herself to Naomi and to the God of Israel.

The two women made the long journey to Bethlehem together. When they arrived, it was the start of the barley harvest. To provide food, Ruth went to gather leftover grain in the fields. As she worked, a man named Boaz noticed her. He was a wealthy landowner and a relative of Naomi's late husband. Boaz had heard of Ruth's loyalty and kindness to Naomi, and he was impressed.

Boaz told his workers to leave extra stalks of grain for Ruth and invited her to eat with them. Naomi was overjoyed when Ruth came home with so much food, and she explained that Boaz was a family redeemer—someone who had the right to marry Ruth and continue the family line.

Guided by Naomi, Ruth humbly approached Boaz, asking him to take her under his protection. Boaz was honored by her request, and though there was another relative with a closer claim, that man declined. Boaz then agreed to marry Ruth.

Their marriage was a blessing not only to Naomi and Ruth but to all Israel. Ruth gave birth to a son named Obed, who became the grandfather of King David. Through Ruth's loyalty and faith, she became part of God's great plan, linking her story to the lineage of Jesus Himself.

- Prayer: Lord, help me be faithful in my relationships and trust Your timing.
- Reflecting Question: When have you had to stay loyal even when it was hard?
- Key Verse: "Where you go I will go, and where you stay I will stay." (Ruth 1:16)
- Faith in Action: Show loyalty this week by supporting a friend or family member.
- Gratitude Prompt: Write one relationship you are thankful for and why.

Samuel Hears God's Voice

The boy Samuel served in the temple under Eli the priest. The days were quiet, and Samuel's duties were simple. He lit lamps, cleaned the sanctuary, and helped Eli as he grew older and weaker. Though Samuel was young, his heart was eager to serve.

One night, the lamps in the temple still burned as Samuel lay down to sleep. The silence was deep, broken only by the faint crackle of the oil lamps. Suddenly, a voice called his name. "Samuel."

He woke and looked around. Thinking Eli had called, Samuel hurried to him and said, "Here I am, you called me."

But Eli shook his head. "I did not call. Go back and lie down."

Samuel returned to his bed. Moments later, the voice came again. "Samuel."

He rose quickly and ran to Eli. "Here I am, you called me."

Eli frowned and replied, "My son, I did not call. Go back and lie down."

Puzzled, Samuel obeyed. Again, the voice called a third time. "Samuel."

The boy ran to Eli once more. "Here I am, you called me."

This time Eli understood. He realized that the Lord was calling the boy. Eli gently told him, "Go and lie down. If He calls you again, say, 'Speak, Lord, for your servant is listening.'"

Samuel returned to his bed, his heart pounding. The stillness seemed heavy with expectation. Then the voice came again, more tender than before. "Samuel, Samuel."

With trembling lips, Samuel answered as Eli had instructed. "Speak, Lord, for your servant is listening." And the Lord spoke to Samuel, revealing His plans and showing him that he had been chosen as a prophet for Israel. From that night forward, Samuel's life was never the same. The boy who once served quietly in the temple now carried the words of God, and the people of Israel would come to know him as a faithful prophet who spoke the truth.

- Prayer: Lord, open my heart to hear Your voice in my life.
- Reflecting Question: How can you make space to listen for God's guidance?
- Key Verse: "Speak, Lord, for your servant is listening." (1 Samuel 3:9)
- Faith in Action: Spend five minutes in silence this week, asking God to guide you.
- Gratitude Prompt: Write one moment when you felt God guiding you.

David and Goliath

David was the youngest son in his family, tasked with tending sheep while his older brothers served in King Saul's army. He spent his days in the hills, playing his harp, watching over the flock, and learning to trust God in solitude. Lions and bears sometimes threatened the sheep, but David had faced them with courage, armed with nothing more than a sling and his faith in the Lord.

One day, Jesse, his father, sent David to the battlefield to bring food to his brothers. When he arrived, he heard the terrifying voice of Goliath, a giant warrior from the Philistines. Every morning and evening, Goliath stepped forward, challenging Israel to send a man to fight him. Covered in armor and carrying a massive spear, he mocked God and filled the Israelites with fear.

The men of Israel shrank back. Even King Saul was afraid. But when David heard Goliath's taunts, something rose up within him. "Who is this man who defies the armies of the living God?" he asked. His brothers scolded him for speaking out, but David's heart burned with faith.

Word of David's courage reached Saul, and he was brought before the king. Saul doubted him at first, but David told him stories of fighting off wild beasts with the Lord's help. "The Lord who rescued me from the paw of the lion and the bear will rescue me from this Philistine," David declared. Reluctantly, Saul agreed. He tried to place his own armor on David, but it was heavy and unfamiliar. David chose instead his staff, sling, and five smooth stones.

As David approached the battlefield, Goliath laughed. "Am I a dog, that you come at me with sticks?" he sneered. But David stood firm. "You come to me with sword and spear, but I come to you in the name of the Lord Almighty, the God of Israel whom you have defied."

The giant moved forward to attack, but David ran quickly toward him. He placed a stone in his sling, whirled it through the air, and struck Goliath square on the forehead. The giant fell face down to the ground. Silence swept across the battlefield before the Philistines turned to flee. Israel's soldiers cheered as their enemy scattered.

David had no armor, no sword, and no experience in battle. What he had was faith. And it was enough to bring victory.

- Prayer: Lord, give me courage to face the giants in my life with faith in You.
- Reflecting Question: What "giant" feels too big in your life right now?
- Key Verse: "The battle is the Lord's." (1 Samuel 17:47)
- Faith in Action: Write down one fear and pray about it each day this week.
- Gratitude Prompt: Thank God for a time He gave you courage.

David and Jonathan's Friendship

Jonathan, the son of King Saul, was a skilled warrior and a respected leader among the soldiers of Israel. David was a shepherd who had risen to fame after defeating Goliath. Though their backgrounds were different, from the first moment they met, Jonathan felt a bond with David. He recognized David's courage and faith in God, and his heart was drawn to him in loyalty and love.

Jonathan made a covenant with David, promising to be his friend for life. As a sign of his devotion, he gave David his robe, his tunic, even his sword, bow, and belt. These were not small gifts. They were symbols of Jonathan's position as the son of the king. By giving them to David, he showed his humility and his willingness to honor God's plan, whatever it might be.

King Saul, however, soon became jealous of David. The people praised David's victories in battle, singing that he had slain tens of thousands, while Saul had slain only thousands. Consumed with envy, Saul began to look at David with suspicion and anger.

Jonathan saw the change in his father's heart and feared for David's life. Though it was not easy to stand against his father, Jonathan remained faithful to his covenant. He warned David when Saul plotted to kill him. He spoke on David's behalf, reminding his father of the good David had done for Israel and how he had risked his life to defeat Goliath.

Saul's jealousy only grew stronger, and his threats against David became more serious. Jonathan and David met in secret to say goodbye. Jonathan told David he must go into hiding until the danger passed. Before they parted, Jonathan reaffirmed his covenant of friendship. They wept together, knowing they might never see each other again.

Later, David would remember Jonathan's loyalty as one of the greatest blessings of his life. Their friendship endured beyond distance, beyond politics, and beyond the hatred of Saul. Jonathan's faithfulness stood as a shining example of what it means to be a true friend.

- Prayer: Lord, help me to be a loyal and faithful friend.
- Reflecting Question: What qualities make someone a true friend?
- Key Verse: "Jonathan made a covenant with David because he loved him as himself." (1 Samuel 18:3)
- Faith in Action: Do something kind for a close friend this week.
- Gratitude Prompt: List two friends you are thankful for and why.

Elijah on Mount Carmel

The land of Israel was dry and cracked, starved of rain for years. Crops withered, rivers shrank, and the people groaned under famine. King Ahab and his wife Jezebel had turned the nation's heart away from the Lord, leading them to worship Baal, a false god who promised rain but brought only silence. In the midst of despair, the prophet Elijah carried a bold challenge from God.

He stood before the king and the people and said, "How long will you waver between two opinions? If the Lord is God, follow Him; but if Baal is God, follow him." The crowd remained silent, caught between fear and uncertainty. Elijah proposed a test: two altars, two sacrifices, no fire. The god who answered with fire would be shown as the true God.

The prophets of Baal prepared their altar first. From morning until noon they shouted, danced, and cried out, "O Baal, answer us!" They slashed themselves with swords until blood flowed, desperate to prove their god's power. But the skies remained still, and no fire came. Elijah mocked them, suggesting Baal was asleep or traveling. The prophets grew louder, but nothing changed. Their altar sat cold and untouched.

When it was Elijah's turn, he rebuilt the altar of the Lord with twelve stones, one for each tribe of Israel. He arranged the wood and placed the sacrifice on top. Then, to remove all doubt, he ordered the people to pour water over the altar, once, twice, and a third time, until the trench around it overflowed. The sacrifice was drenched, the wood dripping wet.

Elijah stepped forward and prayed, "Lord, God of Abraham, Isaac, and Israel, let it be known today that You are God in Israel and that I am Your servant." The moment his prayer ended, fire fell from heaven. It consumed the sacrifice, the wood, the stones, the soil, and even the water in the trench. The people fell to the ground, crying out, "The Lord, He is God! The Lord, He is God!"

That day, God revealed His power unmistakably. The prophets of Baal were silenced, and Israel was reminded of the One who held true authority. Soon after, rain returned to the land, restoring life to a people who had turned away but were called back by God's fire.

- Prayer: Lord, help me stand strong for You even when I feel outnumbered.
- Reflecting Question: When have you felt pressured to follow the crowd?
- Key Verse: "The Lord—he is God! The Lord—he is God!" (1 Kings 18:39)
- Faith in Action: Choose to stand up for your faith in one small way this week.
- Gratitude Prompt: Write one time God showed you His power in your life.

Elijah Hears God in a Whisper

Elijah had just witnessed God's great power on Mount Carmel. Fire had fallen from heaven, consuming the sacrifice and proving that the Lord alone was God. Yet after this victory, Elijah felt weary and afraid. Queen Jezebel threatened to kill him, and the prophet's courage crumbled. He fled into the wilderness, leaving his servant behind, and went a day's journey alone. Exhausted and discouraged, he sat under a broom tree and prayed for his life to end. Sleep came over him, but an angel touched him and told him to eat. Beside him was bread baked over hot coals and a jar of water. Twice the angel returned, urging him to rise and eat, for the journey ahead would be too much without strength. Elijah walked forty days and nights until he reached Mount Horeb, the mountain of God. There he found a cave and stayed the night. The word of the Lord came to him: "What are you doing here, Elijah?" The prophet poured out his heart. He felt alone, hunted, and ready to give up. Then God told him to stand on the mountain in His presence, for the Lord was about to pass by.

Elijah stood at the entrance of the cave. Suddenly a mighty wind tore through the mountains, breaking rocks apart. But the Lord was not in the wind. After the wind came an earthquake that shook the ground beneath his feet. Yet the Lord was not in the earthquake. Then came a fire, blazing and fierce. But the Lord was not in the fire. After the fire came a gentle whisper. When Elijah heard it, he pulled his cloak over his face and stepped out to the cave's entrance. In the stillness of that whisper, he knew he was standing in the presence of God.

Again the voice asked, "What are you doing here, Elijah?" Once more the prophet spoke of his fear and loneliness. But God gave him new direction. He was not alone. There were still thousands in Israel who had not bowed to Baal. Elijah was to rise, return, and continue his mission. Strengthened by the whisper of God, he left the cave ready to walk forward once more.

- Prayer: Lord, help me recognize Your gentle voice in my life and trust You even when I feel afraid.
- Reflecting Question: How do you usually expect God to speak to you, and how might you notice His quiet presence instead?
- Key Verse: "And after the fire came a gentle whisper." (1 Kings 19:12)
- Faith in Action: Spend one quiet moment outdoors this week, turning off distractions and listening for God.
- Gratitude Prompt: Write one simple blessing that brought you peace recently.

Esther's Courage

Esther was a young Jewish woman living in Persia, chosen to become queen after King Xerxes dismissed Queen Vashti. Though she lived in the palace surrounded by luxury, her life was not without danger. Esther had kept her Jewish identity hidden, as her cousin Mordecai had instructed.

One day, a powerful man named Haman rose in the king's court. Haman despised the Jews, especially Mordecai, who refused to bow to him. Filled with rage, Haman devised a plan to destroy all the Jews in the kingdom. He convinced King Xerxes to issue a decree that on a certain day, the Jews could be attacked and killed.

When Mordecai heard of the decree, he was devastated. He tore his clothes, put on sackcloth, and wept in the streets. Through messengers, he begged Esther to go before the king and plead for their people. But Esther was terrified. No one, not even the queen, could approach the king without being summoned. To do so uninvited meant death unless the king extended his golden scepter.

Mordecai's words pressed heavily on Esther's heart. "Do not think that you will escape in the king's palace. Who knows but that you have come to your royal position for such a time as this?" Esther realized that her position was not an accident. She had been placed in the palace for a reason greater than herself. Esther asked Mordecai and the Jewish people to fast for three days, and she and her attendants did the same. On the third day, with her heart pounding, Esther put on her royal robes and went into the inner court. The king looked up, saw Esther, and held out the golden scepter. Her life was spared.

The king asked what troubled her. Esther invited him and Haman to a banquet. At the banquet, she invited them again for a second feast. On the second day, Esther revealed her true identity. She told the king that she was a Jew and that her people were in danger because of Haman's plot. The king was furious. Haman's plan was stopped, and instead of destruction, the Jews were saved.

Through Esther's courage, God delivered His people. She risked her life to do what was right, proving that one person's bravery can change the future of many.

- Prayer: Lord, give me courage to do what is right even when it feels risky.
- Reflecting Question: When was the last time you had to take a stand for what was right?
- Key Verse: "Who knows but that you have come to your royal position for such a time as this?" (Esther 4:14)
- Faith in Action: Speak up this week when you see someone being treated unfairly.
- Gratitude Prompt: Thank God for one time when He gave you courage to act.

Job's Perseverance

Job lived in the land of Uz and was known as a man of integrity. He feared God and turned away from evil. He was wealthy, with thousands of livestock, many servants, and a large family. People respected him, not just for his riches but for his devotion to God.

One day, a series of disasters struck Job's life. His servants rushed to him with terrible news. Raiders had stolen his oxen and donkeys. Fire from the sky burned his sheep. Enemy bands carried off his camels. Worst of all, a violent wind collapsed the house where his sons and daughters were feasting, and they all died. In the span of one day, Job lost everything he treasured.

Grief tore through Job, but he did not curse God. He fell to the ground and said, "The Lord gave, and the Lord has taken away; blessed be the name of the Lord." Though his heart was broken, his faith held firm.

Later, Job's suffering deepened. Painful sores broke out on his body, from the soles of his feet to the crown of his head. He sat in ashes, scraping himself with a piece of pottery, a shadow of the man he once was. His wife told him to give up and curse God, but Job replied, "Shall we accept good from God, and not trouble?"

Three friends came to comfort him, but instead of easing his pain they accused him. They said his suffering must be punishment for hidden sins. Job defended his innocence, insisting he had done nothing to deserve such misery. He wrestled with questions, cried out to God, and longed for answers. Yet even in his confusion, Job never abandoned his faith.

After a long season of silence, God spoke to Job out of a whirlwind. He reminded Job of His power as Creator, the One who laid the foundations of the earth and commands the seas. Job realized that God's wisdom was beyond his understanding. Humbled, he repented for questioning God's plan.

In the end, God restored Job's fortunes. He gave him twice as much as before, more livestock, more wealth, and ten more children. Job lived a long life, full of days, and saw his children's children. His story became a testimony that faith can endure even the darkest trials, and that God's purposes are never wasted.

- Prayer: Lord, help me trust You even in times of pain and confusion.
- Reflecting Question: How do you usually react when life feels unfair?
- Key Verse: "Though he slay me, yet will I hope in him." (Job 13:15)
- Faith in Action: Encourage someone who is going through a tough time.
- Gratitude Prompt: Write one blessing you sometimes take for granted.

Daniel in the Lions' Den

Daniel had risen to a place of great influence in the kingdom of Babylon. Because of his wisdom and integrity, King Darius trusted him more than all the other officials. Daniel stood out among them, and the king planned to set him over the entire kingdom.

The other administrators grew jealous. They searched for some fault in Daniel's work, but he was honest and faithful in everything. Finally, they realized the only way to accuse him was through his devotion to God. They convinced King Darius to sign a law that for thirty days no one could pray to any god or person except the king himself. Whoever disobeyed would be thrown into a den of lions.

When Daniel heard about the law, he went home, opened his windows toward Jerusalem, and prayed three times a day just as he had always done. His enemies were waiting. They rushed to tell the king that Daniel had broken the law.

King Darius was deeply troubled. He respected Daniel and did not want to harm him, but the law of the Medes and Persians could not be changed. Reluctantly, the king ordered Daniel to be thrown into the den of lions. Before the stone was rolled across the entrance, the king said, "May your God, whom you serve continually, rescue you."

That night, the king could not eat or sleep. At dawn, he hurried to the den and cried out, "Daniel, servant of the living God, has your God been able to rescue you from the lions?"

From inside came Daniel's voice: "My God sent his angel, and he shut the mouths of the lions. They have not hurt me, because I was found innocent in his sight."

The king was overjoyed. He ordered Daniel lifted from the den, and not a single wound was found on him because he had trusted in God. Then the king issued a new decree that everyone in his kingdom must fear and honor the God of Daniel, for He is the living God who endures forever.

- Prayer: Lord, strengthen my faith to stand firm no matter the cost.
- Reflecting Question: What might make you afraid to show your faith openly?
- Key Verse: "My God sent his angel, and he shut the mouths of the lions." (Daniel 6:22)
- Faith in Action: Pray boldly in a place where you normally stay silent.
- Gratitude Prompt: Thank God for one time He kept you safe.

Shadrach, Meshach, and Abednego in the Fiery Furnace

King Nebuchadnezzar built a massive golden statue and commanded that at the sound of music all people should bow and worship it. Anyone who refused would be thrown into a blazing furnace. The decree spread across Babylon, and when the music played, crowds fell to their knees. Yet three young men, Shadrach, Meshach, and Abednego, remained standing tall.

The king's officials quickly reported them. Furious, Nebuchadnezzar summoned the three and gave them one last chance. "If you do not bow when the music plays, you will be cast into the furnace. Then what god will be able to rescue you from my hand?"

The young men answered with calm courage. "O king, we do not need to defend ourselves before you. If we are thrown into the blazing furnace, the God we serve is able to save us. But even if He does not, we will not serve your gods or worship the image you have set up."

Nebuchadnezzar's face darkened with rage. He ordered the furnace heated seven times hotter than usual. His strongest soldiers tied Shadrach, Meshach, and Abednego and threw them into the flames. The fire was so fierce that it killed the men who carried them in.

Inside the furnace, something miraculous happened. The three young men walked freely among the flames, unharmed. Nebuchadnezzar leapt to his feet in astonishment. "Did we not throw three men bound into the fire? Look! I see four men walking in the fire, unbound and unharmed, and the fourth looks like a son of the gods."

The king rushed to the furnace door and shouted, "Shadrach, Meshach, and Abednego, servants of the Most High God, come out!" The young men stepped out. The fire had not harmed their bodies, their hair was not singed, their robes were not scorched, and there was not even the smell of fire on them.

Nebuchadnezzar praised their God. "Blessed be the God of Shadrach, Meshach, and Abednego, who has sent His angel and delivered His servants. They trusted Him and defied my command. No other god can save in this way." From that day, the courage of three faithful men became a lasting testimony of trust in God's power.

- Prayer: Lord, give me courage to stand for You even when I face pressure.
- Reflecting Question: What situations make it hard for you to live out your faith?
- Key Verse: "The God we serve is able to deliver us from it, and he will deliver us from Your Majesty's hand." (Daniel 3:17)
- Faith in Action: Choose one small area where you are tempted to compromise and stand firm this week.
- Gratitude Prompt: Thank God for one time He protected or strengthened you in a difficult situation.

Jonah and the Great Fish

Jonah was a prophet of the Lord, known among his people for carrying God's messages. One day, God gave Jonah a command that startled him. He was told to go to the great city of Nineveh and preach against its wickedness. Jonah knew the reputation of Nineveh. It was a powerful city, filled with cruelty and violence, and he did not want to go. Instead of obeying, Jonah decided to flee in the opposite direction.

He traveled to the port city of Joppa and found a ship bound for Tarshish, far away from Nineveh. He paid his fare and boarded, thinking he could escape from God's presence. As the ship sailed into the open sea, a violent storm arose. Waves crashed against the vessel, and the sailors feared it would break apart. They prayed to their gods and threw cargo overboard to lighten the load, but nothing helped.

Jonah, meanwhile, was below deck, asleep. The captain woke him and urged him to pray to his God. The sailors cast lots to discover who was responsible for the disaster, and the lot fell on Jonah. He admitted that he was running away from the Lord, the God who made the sea and the land. The sailors were terrified. Jonah told them that the only way to calm the storm was to throw him into the sea.

Reluctantly, the men lifted Jonah and cast him into the raging waters. Immediately the storm grew calm. The sailors were amazed, and they offered sacrifices to the Lord. Jonah, sinking into the deep, felt the waters surround him. Just as he was about to drown, God provided a great fish that swallowed him whole.

Inside the belly of the fish, Jonah remained for three days and three nights. In that darkness, he prayed to God with a repentant heart. He confessed his disobedience and thanked the Lord for saving his life. God heard his prayer and commanded the fish to release Jonah. The fish vomited him onto dry land.

Once again, God spoke to Jonah: "Go to Nineveh and proclaim the message I give you." This time, Jonah obeyed. He walked into the great city and delivered God's warning. To Jonah's surprise, the people listened. From the king down to the commoner, they humbled themselves, fasted, and turned from their evil ways. God saw their repentance and spared the city from destruction.

- Prayer: Lord, help me obey quickly instead of running from Your plans.
- Reflecting Question: Have you ever tried to avoid doing what you knew was right?
- Key Verse: "Salvation comes from the Lord." (Jonah 2:9)
- Faith in Action: Do one act of obedience this week, even if it feels difficult.
- Gratitude Prompt: Thank God for His patience and second chances.

The Call of Isaiah

The year was marked by sorrow as King Uzziah had died, and the people of Judah were uncertain about their future. In the midst of this grief and unrest, Isaiah entered the temple. He came as he had many times before, but this day would be unlike any other.

As Isaiah stepped inside, his eyes were lifted upward, and what he saw filled him with awe. The Lord was seated on a high and exalted throne, and the train of His robe filled the temple. Above Him stood mighty seraphim, each with six wings. With two they covered their faces, with two they covered their feet, and with two they flew. They cried out to one another in voices that shook the very foundations of the temple: "Holy, holy, holy is the Lord Almighty; the whole earth is full of His glory."

Smoke filled the house of God, and Isaiah fell to his knees. The weight of the moment pressed down upon him, and he became painfully aware of his own sin. "Woe to me," he cried. "I am ruined! For I am a man of unclean lips, and I live among a people of unclean lips, yet my eyes have seen the King, the Lord Almighty."

As the words left his mouth, one of the seraphim flew toward him, carrying a live coal taken from the altar with tongs. The angel touched the coal to Isaiah's lips and said, "See, this has touched your lips; your guilt is taken away and your sin atoned for." The burning sensation was not of pain but of cleansing, and Isaiah's heart was filled with peace.

Then came a voice, clear and powerful, echoing through the temple: "Whom shall I send, and who will go for us?"

Isaiah, trembling yet transformed, knew this was the reason he had been brought into God's presence. His fear gave way to courage, and his shame to readiness. He answered without hesitation, "Here am I. Send me!"

The vision ended, but Isaiah's life had changed forever. He had encountered the holiness of God, received forgiveness, and embraced his calling. From that day forward, Isaiah would carry God's message to the people, no matter the cost.

- Prayer: Lord, make me willing to serve You wherever You call me.
- Reflecting Question: What holds you back from saying "yes" to God?
- Key Verse: "Here am I. Send me!" (Isaiah 6:8)
- Faith in Action: Volunteer for one act of service this week.
- Gratitude Prompt: Thank God for giving you gifts and opportunities to serve.

The Valley of Dry Bones

The hand of the Lord came upon Ezekiel and carried him in the Spirit to a valley filled with bones. Everywhere he looked, the ground was scattered with dry, lifeless remains. They were not just bones of a few, but of a vast multitude. The sight was haunting, a silent testimony of hopelessness and defeat.

God asked Ezekiel, "Son of man, can these bones live?" Ezekiel, overwhelmed by the vision, answered, "Sovereign Lord, You alone know."

Then God told him to prophesy over the bones. Ezekiel obeyed and began to speak the words given to him: "Dry bones, hear the word of the Lord. I will make breath enter you, and you will come to life." As he spoke, a great noise shook the valley. The bones began to rattle and come together, bone to bone. Sinews appeared, then flesh, and finally skin covered them. Yet they lay still, without breath.

God said again, "Prophesy to the breath; prophesy, son of man, and say: 'Come, breath, from the four winds and breathe into these slain, that they may live.'" Ezekiel spoke, and the breath entered them. Suddenly the valley was filled with living men, standing on their feet, an exceedingly great army.

Then the Lord explained the vision. "Son of man, these bones are the people of Israel. They say, 'Our bones are dried up and our hope is gone; we are cut off.' But I will open their graves and bring them up from them. I will bring them back to the land of Israel. I will put my Spirit in them, and they will live."

The promise was clear: God would restore His people. Where there was only despair, He would bring life. Where there was emptiness, He would breathe hope again. Ezekiel stood in awe, knowing that the God of Israel was not only Lord over the living but also Lord over death itself.

- Prayer: Lord, breathe new life into the parts of my heart that feel empty and hopeless.
- Reflecting Question: What part of your life feels lifeless and needs God's renewal?
- Key Verse: "I will put my Spirit in you and you will live." (Ezekiel 37:14)
- Faith in Action: Spend time in prayer asking God to renew one area of your life this week.
- Gratitude Prompt: Thank God for one time He gave you strength when you felt weak.

The Birth of Jesus

The night was quiet in the little town of Bethlehem. Houses and inns were full because people had traveled from far and wide for the census ordered by Caesar Augustus. Among the travelers were Joseph and Mary, a young woman chosen by God to carry His Son. The journey had been long and tiring, and Mary was ready to give birth.

When they arrived in Bethlehem, there was no room for them anywhere. Every door Joseph knocked on was closed. Finally, someone offered them a simple place where animals were kept. It was far from comfortable, but it was shelter. There, surrounded by straw and the warmth of the animals, Mary gave birth to her firstborn son. She wrapped Him in cloths and placed Him in a manger, a feeding trough for livestock. This was not the grand entrance of a king that the world expected, but it was exactly how God planned His Son to arrive.

Out in the fields nearby, shepherds were keeping watch over their flocks. They were ordinary men doing their nightly work, unaware that their lives were about to change forever. Suddenly, the sky lit up with the glory of the Lord. An angel appeared and the shepherds were terrified. But the angel said, "Do not be afraid. I bring you good news of great joy that will be for all the people. Today in the town of David a Savior has been born to you. He is Christ the Lord." Then the angel told them how to find Him: a baby wrapped in cloths and lying in a manger.

Before the shepherds could even speak, a vast company of heavenly angels appeared, praising God and saying, "Glory to God in the highest, and on earth peace to those on whom His favor rests." The night sky rang with their voices, and the shepherds stood in awe. When the angels left, the shepherds said to each other, "Let's go to Bethlehem and see this thing that has happened." Without hesitation, they hurried to find Mary, Joseph, and the baby.

They found the newborn lying in the manger, just as the angel had said. Their hearts overflowed with wonder. After seeing Him, they spread the word about what they had been told concerning this child, and everyone who heard it was amazed. The shepherds returned to their fields, glorifying and praising God for all the things they had seen and heard. The Savior had come, and hope had entered the world.

- Prayer: Lord, thank You for sending Jesus into the world as the greatest gift of all. Fill my heart with the same joy the shepherds felt that night.
- Reflecting Question: How does the humble birth of Jesus show God's love for you?
- Key Verse: "I bring you good news that will cause great joy for all the people." (Luke 2:10)
- Faith in Action: Share the joy of Jesus' birth with a friend or family member this week.
- Gratitude Prompt: Write down three blessings you are thankful for this Christmas season.

The Boy Jesus in the Temple

Every year, Joseph and Mary traveled from Nazareth to Jerusalem for the Feast of the Passover. It was a long journey, filled with the noise of families, songs of praise, and the steady rhythm of footsteps. When Jesus was twelve years old, He joined them on this pilgrimage, walking alongside the caravan of relatives and neighbors.

The feast days were filled with awe. The streets of Jerusalem overflowed with worshippers, priests performed sacrifices, and the air carried the scent of incense from the temple. Jesus' eyes shone with curiosity as He watched and listened. Everything about the temple stirred His heart with wonder.

When the feast ended, the caravan began its return to Nazareth. Families gathered their belongings, children played at the edges of the crowd, and parents assumed everyone was safe among relatives. Joseph and Mary walked with the travelers, confident that Jesus was nearby.

But as the day ended and they stopped for the night, their hearts filled with sudden fear. Jesus was not with His cousins. He was not with friends. They searched frantically through the camp, calling His name, but no answer came. Anxiety gripped them. Their boy was missing.

The next morning they hurried back to Jerusalem. For three days they searched the crowded streets, markets, and gathering places. Finally, they entered the temple courts. There He was. Jesus sat among the teachers, His face calm and focused. He listened intently, asking questions that revealed wisdom far beyond His years. The teachers marveled at His understanding and the depth of His answers.

Mary rushed forward, relief washing over her fear. "Son, why have You treated us like this? Your father and I have been anxiously searching for You."

Jesus looked at her with quiet certainty. "Why were you searching for Me? Didn't you know I had to be in My Father's house?" Mary and Joseph did not fully understand His words, but they treasured them in their hearts. Jesus returned home with them to Nazareth, obedient to His parents, and He continued to grow. With each passing year, He matured in wisdom, gained strength, and found favor with both God and people. The boy who amazed the teachers in the temple was preparing for a mission that would one day change the world.

- Prayer: Lord, give me a heart eager to learn and grow in Your Word.
- Reflecting Question: How can you grow in wisdom and faith like Jesus did?
- Key Verse: "And Jesus grew in wisdom and stature, and in favor with God and man." (Luke 2:52)
- Faith in Action: Spend extra time this week reading a Bible passage on your own.
- Gratitude Prompt: Thank God for one teacher or mentor in your life.

The Baptism of Jesus

The Jordan River flowed steadily under the warm sun, its waters glistening as people gathered along the banks. They had come from towns and villages, drawn by the voice of a prophet named John. He preached a message of repentance, urging everyone to prepare their hearts for the coming of God's kingdom. Clothed in rough camel's hair and living simply in the wilderness, John baptized those who confessed their sins, lowering them into the water and raising them up as a sign of a new beginning. Among the crowd that day was Jesus of Nazareth. He had grown up quietly in Galilee, known to most as the carpenter's son. Few realized the full purpose of His life, but now the moment had come for Him to step into His public mission. Without hesitation, He approached John and asked to be baptized.

John was taken aback. He looked into Jesus' eyes and saw no guilt, no sin that needed cleansing. "I should be baptized by You," John said, his voice filled with awe. "And yet You come to me?"

Jesus answered with calm certainty. "Let it be so now. It is proper for us to do this to fulfill all righteousness." Though He was sinless, Jesus chose to identify with the people He had come to save, stepping fully into their humanity and obedience to God.

John consented. He led Jesus into the Jordan and gently lowered Him beneath the surface. The cool water closed over Him, then released Him as He rose again, water streaming from His hair and robes. In that instant, something extraordinary happened.

The heavens opened above the river, and the Spirit of God descended like a dove, resting upon Him with quiet grace. A voice echoed from above, clear and powerful, filling the hearts of everyone present. "This is my Son, whom I love; with Him I am well pleased."

The crowd stood in hushed amazement. Jesus did not seek recognition or applause. Instead, He stood humbly, filled with the Spirit, ready to begin the mission that would change the world. His baptism was more than a ritual. It was the beginning of His journey to bring light, healing, and salvation to all who would believe.

- Prayer: Lord, remind me that I am Your beloved child too.
- Reflecting Question: What does it mean to you to be called God's child?
- Key Verse: "This is my Son, whom I love; with him I am well pleased." (Matthew 3:17)
- Faith in Action: Encourage someone by reminding them of their worth in God's eyes.
- Gratitude Prompt: Write down one reason you are thankful for your identity in Christ.

The Temptation of Jesus

After His baptism in the Jordan River, Jesus was led by the Spirit into the wilderness. For forty days and forty nights He ate nothing, choosing to fast and draw close to His Father. The sun burned during the day, the nights were cold, and the silence was heavy. Hunger gnawed at Him until He grew weak. Still, His heart was steady in prayer.

It was then that the tempter came. The devil knew Jesus was hungry and pointed to the smooth stones scattered across the ground. "If You are the Son of God, command these stones to become bread." The suggestion seemed simple. Jesus had the power. But He refused to use it for selfish gain. Looking at the enemy, He answered with words from Scripture: "Man shall not live on bread alone, but on every word that comes from the mouth of God."

The devil led Him to the holy city and placed Him at the highest point of the temple. Looking down at the crowds far below, the enemy whispered, "If You are the Son of God, throw Yourself down. For it is written: He will command His angels concerning You, and they will lift You up in their hands, so that You will not strike Your foot against a stone." The words twisted Scripture into a dare, tempting Jesus to prove Himself through a dramatic display. But Jesus would not play that game. Calmly, He replied, "It is also written: Do not put the Lord your God to the test."

Finally, the devil took Jesus to a very high mountain. He showed Him all the kingdoms of the world, their wealth, their glory, and their power. The devil's voice grew urgent. "All this I will give You if You will bow down and worship me." For a moment, the world stretched out before Jesus, dazzling and shining. But His heart belonged to His Father alone. He turned to the devil with authority and declared, "Away from me, Satan! For it is written: Worship the Lord your God, and serve Him only." At those words, the devil fled. The wilderness grew still again. Soon angels came to Jesus and ministered to Him, bringing comfort and strength after His long trial.

- Prayer: Lord, help me resist temptation and stand firm in Your truth.
- Reflecting Question: What temptation do you face most often, and how can God's Word help you overcome it?
- Key Verse: "Man shall not live on bread alone, but on every word that comes from the mouth of God." (Matthew 4:4)
- Faith in Action: Memorize one Bible verse this week to use when you feel tempted.
- Gratitude Prompt: Thank God for giving you strength to resist even the small temptations in daily life.

The Calling of the First Disciples

The sun was rising over the Sea of Galilee, casting a golden light across the waves. Fishermen moved about their boats, pulling in empty nets after a long night without success. Among them were two brothers, Simon, called Peter, and Andrew. Their arms were tired, their faces lined with frustration. They had worked hard, yet the nets were bare.

As they cleaned their gear on the shore, a man approached. His presence carried both gentleness and authority. It was Jesus. He stepped onto their boat and asked Peter to push out a little from the land. Sitting down, Jesus taught the crowd that had gathered, His words carried across the water like the steady rhythm of the waves. When He finished speaking, He turned to Peter. "Put out into deep water, and let down the nets for a catch." Peter hesitated. He knew the sea well. They had tried all night and caught nothing. Still, something about Jesus compelled him. "Master, we've worked hard all night and haven't caught anything. But because you say so, I will let down the nets."

Together, Peter and Andrew lowered their nets once more. Suddenly, the ropes grew heavy. The water churned with fish, so many that the nets began to break. They signaled their partners, James and John, the sons of Zebedee, to bring another boat. Both boats filled to the point of nearly sinking.

Amazement struck the fishermen. Peter fell to his knees before Jesus. "Go away from me, Lord. I am a sinful man!"

But Jesus lifted him up with calm assurance. "Don't be afraid. From now on you will fish for people."

The brothers looked at one another, their hearts pounding with both fear and wonder. The boats, once their livelihood, now seemed small compared to the calling before them. They pulled them ashore, leaving behind the catch of a lifetime. With nets abandoned and boats resting on the sand, Peter, Andrew, James, and John walked after Jesus. From that day forward, their lives would never be the same.

- Prayer: Lord, help me follow You with a willing heart, even when it means leaving behind what feels secure.
- Reflecting Question: What might God be asking you to leave behind in order to follow Him more fully?
- Key Verse: "Come, follow me, and I will send you out to fish for people." (Matthew 4:19)
- Faith in Action: Take one small step of obedience this week in your faith, even if it feels uncertain.
- Gratitude Prompt: Write one way following Jesus has changed your life for the better.

The Sermon on the Mount

Crowds gathered on the hillside, eager to hear from Jesus. Families pressed close together, children sat on the grass, and fishermen left their nets to listen. The people had heard of his miracles and longed for his words of life. As Jesus climbed higher and sat down, a hush fell over the crowd. His disciples drew near, their eyes fixed on him.

Jesus began to speak. His voice was steady, carrying across the hill, gentle yet filled with authority. "Blessed are the poor in spirit, for theirs is the kingdom of heaven. Blessed are those who mourn, for they will be comforted. Blessed are the meek, for they will inherit the earth." The words struck the people's hearts, overturning what they thought strength and blessing meant.

He spoke of mercy and purity of heart, of peacemakers being called children of God. He told them that those who faced insults and persecution because of righteousness were not cursed, but blessed. Every phrase was like water on thirsty ground. People leaned forward, realizing he was not teaching like the religious leaders they knew.

Jesus lifted their gaze higher. "You are the light of the world. A city on a hill cannot be hidden. Let your light shine before others, that they may see your good deeds and glorify your Father in heaven." The crowd shifted as they realized he was calling them to live differently, to be salt and light in a broken world.

He explained that he had not come to abolish the law, but to fulfill it. He spoke of anger, forgiveness, love for enemies, prayer in secret, trusting God instead of worrying, and building a life on obedience to his words. His teaching was bold and challenging, yet filled with hope.

As the sun dipped lower, his words settled deeply into the hearts of those listening. Some nodded in agreement, others wrestled silently with the weight of his message. But all knew they had heard something unlike anything before. Jesus had painted a picture of a new way to live, one that brought heaven close to earth.

When Jesus finished, the crowd remained in awe. They had come seeking a teacher, but they left knowing they had been in the presence of one who spoke with the authority of God himself.

- Prayer: Lord, help me live out Your teachings with humility and love.
- Reflecting Question: Which Beatitude speaks most to your life right now?
- Key Verse: "Blessed are the pure in heart, for they will see God." (Matthew 5:8)
- Faith in Action: Practice one Beatitude this week in a concrete way.
- Gratitude Prompt: Thank God for one way He has blessed you recently.

Jesus Calms the Storm

The sun was setting over the Sea of Galilee as Jesus told His disciples, "Let us go over to the other side." They left the crowd behind and set out in a boat. The water was calm at first, and the cool night breeze carried them forward. Some of the disciples, experienced fishermen, guided the boat with steady hands. Others sat quietly, grateful for the chance to rest after a long day of teaching.

As the boat moved farther from the shore, dark clouds began to gather. The wind picked up, stronger with each passing moment. Soon waves rose high, crashing against the boat and filling it with water. The disciples struggled to keep control, their voices rising in fear. The storm howled all around them, and even the seasoned fishermen felt powerless.

Meanwhile, Jesus was in the stern, asleep on a cushion. While the storm raged, He rested peacefully. The disciples could hardly believe it. Desperation overcame them, and they woke Him, shouting, "Teacher, don't you care if we drown?" Their hearts pounded with terror as the boat pitched back and forth.

Jesus stood up, facing the wind and the waves. He raised His voice above the storm, saying simply, "Quiet! Be still!" At once the wind died down, and the sea became completely calm. The silence that followed was almost as overwhelming as the storm itself. The disciples stared in awe, their fear shifting into amazement.

Jesus turned to them and asked, "Why are you so afraid? Do you still have no faith?" His words cut through the quiet, leaving them to ponder the meaning. They whispered among themselves, "Who is this? Even the wind and the waves obey Him!"

In that moment, the disciples realized they were in the presence of someone far greater than they had imagined. The storm that had filled them with dread was no match for the authority of Jesus. His power brought peace where there had been chaos, and safety where there had been danger.

The boat continued across the calm sea under the starlit sky. The disciples sat in awe, their fear replaced by wonder. They would not forget this night, when the One they followed revealed that even nature itself bowed to His command.

- Prayer: Lord, calm the storms in my heart and remind me that You are always in control.
- Reflecting Question: What fears in your life feel like storms that overwhelm you?
- Key Verse: "Even the wind and the waves obey him." (Mark 4:41)
- Faith in Action: When you feel anxious this week, stop and pray instead of letting fear take over.
- Gratitude Prompt: Thank God for one time He gave you peace in the middle of a difficult situation.

The Feeding of the 5,000

The day had been long, and the crowds showed no sign of leaving. Jesus had been teaching near the Sea of Galilee, and people had followed Him from the towns and villages. Men, women, and children gathered on the grassy hillside, listening to His words and watching as He healed the sick. Their eyes were fixed on Him, hungry for hope and truth.

As evening approached, the disciples grew anxious. They knew the people had been there all day without food. Philip voiced the concern that weighed on all their hearts. "Where shall we buy bread for these people to eat?" Even if they had months of wages, it would not be enough to feed such a multitude.

Andrew stepped forward, hesitant but hopeful. He had noticed a boy in the crowd carrying a small lunch, just five barley loaves and two small fish. It was little more than a snack, nothing compared to the needs of thousands. Still, he brought it to Jesus. "Here is a boy with five small loaves and two fish," Andrew said, "but how far will they go among so many?"

Jesus looked at the boy, then at the crowd stretching across the hillside. He took the meager offering in His hands. "Have the people sit down," He instructed. The disciples moved through the crowd, arranging the people in groups. The grassy slope filled with clusters of families and friends sitting expectantly.

Jesus lifted the loaves and fish toward heaven and gave thanks. Then He began breaking the bread and dividing the fish. He placed portions in the hands of the disciples, who in turn carried them to the waiting people. They returned again and again, and still the food did not run out. The small meal grew into a feast as baskets overflowed with bread and fish.

The people ate until they were satisfied, every last one of them. Children laughed with full stomachs, and families marveled at what had taken place before their eyes. The disciples, who had doubted only moments earlier, gathered up twelve baskets of leftovers. What began as a boy's simple gift had become a miracle that fed thousands. As the sun dipped low and the crowd prepared to leave, the hillside was alive with awe. The people knew they had witnessed something extraordinary, a glimpse of heaven's abundance given through the hands of Jesus.

- Prayer: Lord, thank You for providing more than enough in my life. Help me trust You with what little I have.
- Reflecting Question: When have you seen something small become more than enough?
- Key Verse: "Jesus then took the loaves, gave thanks, and distributed to those who were seated." (John 6:11)
- Faith in Action: Share something you have with someone this week, even if it feels small.
- Gratitude Prompt: List three ways God has provided for you recently.

Jesus Walks on Water

After feeding thousands with just a few loaves and fish, Jesus told His disciples to get into the boat and go ahead of Him across the Sea of Galilee. As evening came, He went up on a mountainside alone to pray. The boat was already far from shore, and the disciples were straining at the oars as the wind blew fiercely against them.

The waves rose high, and the night grew darker. The disciples battled the storm, tired and afraid. In the early hours of the morning, Jesus came toward them, walking on the water. The disciples cried out in fear, thinking they saw a ghost. But immediately Jesus spoke to them, "Take courage! It is I. Don't be afraid."

Peter, hearing the familiar voice, called back, "Lord, if it is really You, tell me to come to You on the water." Jesus answered simply, "Come."

Peter stepped out of the boat. For a moment, he walked on the waves, his eyes fixed on Jesus. But then he noticed the wind, saw the water swirling beneath his feet, and fear rushed in. Doubt overcame his faith, and he began to sink. "Lord, save me!" he shouted.

Jesus reached out His hand immediately and caught him. "You of little faith," He said, "why did you doubt?" Together they climbed into the boat, and as soon as they did, the wind died down. The storm was gone, replaced by stillness.

The disciples were overwhelmed. They bowed before Jesus, saying, "Truly You are the Son of God." What they had witnessed was unlike anything they had seen before. Jesus had shown them His power over creation and His care for them in their fear.

That night, their faith deepened. They realized that even in the fiercest storm, Jesus was present. He had not abandoned them, and He had proven once again that He was truly the Lord.

- Prayer: Lord, help me keep my eyes on You when I feel afraid, and remind me that You are greater than my fears.
- Reflecting Question: What fears distract you from trusting God fully?
- Key Verse: "Take courage! It is I. Don't be afraid." (Matthew 14:27)
- Faith in Action: Write down one fear you are facing this week and pray over it each day.
- Gratitude Prompt: Thank God for a time He lifted you up when you felt like sinking.

The Good Samaritan

A teacher of the law once stood up to test Jesus. "Teacher," he asked, "what must I do to inherit eternal life?" Jesus answered with a question: "What is written in the Law? How do you read it?" The man replied, "Love the Lord your God with all your heart and with all your soul and with all your strength and with all your mind, and love your neighbor as yourself."

"You have answered correctly," Jesus said. "Do this and you will live."

But the man wanted to justify himself, so he asked, "And who is my neighbor?"

Jesus told him a story.

A man was traveling from Jerusalem down to Jericho. Along the way, robbers attacked him. They stripped him of his clothes, beat him, and left him half dead on the side of the road.

By chance a priest came along. When he saw the wounded man, he crossed to the other side of the road and kept going. Soon after, a Levite came by. He too saw the man lying there, but he also passed on the other side.

Finally, a Samaritan came along the same road. The Jews and Samaritans were enemies, but when the Samaritan saw the man, his heart was moved with compassion. He went to him, bandaged his wounds, pouring on oil and wine. He lifted the man onto his own donkey and brought him to an inn, where he cared for him through the night.

The next day, the Samaritan gave two silver coins to the innkeeper. "Take care of him," he said, "and when I return, I will pay back any extra expenses."

After telling the story, Jesus asked the teacher of the law, "Which of these three do you think was a neighbor to the man who fell into the hands of robbers?"

The teacher replied, "The one who had mercy on him."

Jesus said, "Go and do likewise."

- Prayer: Lord, give me compassion to care for others, no matter who they are.
- Reflecting Question: Who in your life might need your kindness right now?
- Key Verse: "Love your neighbor as yourself." (Luke 10:27)
- Faith in Action: Do one act of kindness this week for someone outside your circle of friends.
- Gratitude Prompt: Thank God for someone who showed you unexpected kindness.

The Prodigal Son

A man had two sons. The younger one grew restless and demanded his share of the inheritance. Though his father's heart was heavy, he divided the property between them. Not long after, the younger son gathered all he had and set off for a distant country.

There he lived recklessly, spending his wealth on pleasures that did not last. With each passing day, his purse grew lighter until it was empty. When a severe famine struck the land, he had nothing left. Hungry and desperate, he found work feeding pigs, so poor that he longed to eat the food given to them.

In his misery, he thought of his father's house. Even the servants there had bread enough to spare. He said to himself, "I will return to my father and say, 'Father, I have sinned against heaven and against you. I am no longer worthy to be called your son. Make me like one of your hired servants.'"

So he rose and began the long journey home. As he approached the village, weak and ashamed, his father saw him from far away. Compassion filled the father's heart, and he ran to his son. He embraced him tightly, holding him as if to never let go. The son began his speech, but the father called to the servants, "Quick, bring the best robe and put it on him. Place a ring on his finger and sandals on his feet. Prepare the fattened calf. We must celebrate, for this son of mine was dead and is alive again; he was lost and is found."

Music and joy filled the house as the feast began. Yet the older son, who had been working in the field, heard the celebration and grew angry. He refused to go in. His father came out to him, but the older son said, "All these years I have served you faithfully and never disobeyed, yet you never gave me even a young goat to celebrate with my friends. But when this son of yours returns after wasting everything, you honor him with a feast."

The father gently replied, "My son, you are always with me, and everything I have is yours. But we had to celebrate and be glad, because your brother was dead and is alive again; he was lost and is found."

- Prayer: Lord, thank You for always welcoming me back with open arms when I fail.
- Reflecting Question: How do you respond when someone asks for forgiveness?
- Key Verse: "This son of mine was dead and is alive again; he was lost and is found." (Luke 15:24)
- Faith in Action: Choose one person to forgive this week, even if it feels hard.
- Gratitude Prompt: Write down one way God has shown you mercy and grace.

The Rich Young Ruler

A young man approached Jesus one day as He was setting out on a journey. The man was wealthy and respected, yet his heart was unsettled. He ran to Jesus, knelt before Him, and asked, "Good Teacher, what must I do to inherit eternal life?"

Jesus looked at him with calm eyes and replied, "Why do you call me good? No one is good except God alone. You know the commandments: do not murder, do not commit adultery, do not steal, do not give false testimony, do not defraud, honor your father and mother."

The young man straightened his back and answered with confidence, "Teacher, all these I have kept since I was a boy." He had worked hard to live a life of obedience, and he expected Jesus to commend him.

Instead, Jesus looked at him with love and spoke words that pierced the man's heart. "You still lack one thing. Go, sell everything you have and give to the poor, and you will have treasure in heaven. Then come, follow me." The words hung in the air. The young man's face fell. He had great wealth, and his possessions had always been a source of pride and security. To let them go felt impossible. He wanted eternal life, but he was unwilling to release what bound him most tightly. With sorrow in his eyes, he turned and walked away.

Jesus watched him go and then turned to His disciples. "How hard it is for the rich to enter the kingdom of God!" The disciples were astonished, so He explained again, "Children, how hard it is to enter the kingdom of God. It is easier for a camel to go through the eye of a needle than for someone who is rich to enter the kingdom of God."

The disciples whispered among themselves, "Who then can be saved?" Their question was filled with fear, for they wondered if anyone could ever meet such a standard. Jesus fixed His gaze on them and said, "With man this is impossible, but not with God. All things are possible with God." The lesson was clear. Eternal life was not something earned by keeping rules or holding onto wealth. It was a gift, received by those willing to follow Jesus with open hands and surrendered hearts.

- Prayer: Lord, help me value You above all my possessions and desires.
- Reflecting Question: What's one thing you might be holding on to more than God?
- Key Verse: "With man this is impossible, but not with God; all things are possible with God." (Mark 10:27)
- Faith in Action: Give up one small comfort this week to focus more on God.
- Gratitude Prompt: Thank God for what you already have instead of what you lack.

Zacchaeus the Tax Collector

Zacchaeus was a man who lived in the city of Jericho. He worked as a chief tax collector, which made him wealthy but also unpopular. People in his town despised him because tax collectors often cheated others and were seen as traitors, working for the Romans. Zacchaeus had money, but he did not have respect or true friendship.

One day, news spread through Jericho that Jesus was coming to town. Crowds filled the streets, eager to see the teacher and miracle worker. Zacchaeus, curious but also desperate for something more in life, wanted to see Jesus for himself. There was a problem. Zacchaeus was short, and the crowd blocked his view. No one wanted to let him through.

Determined not to miss the moment, Zacchaeus ran ahead and climbed into a sycamore tree that stood along the road where Jesus would pass. From the branches, he could finally see above the crowd. As Jesus came closer, Zacchaeus leaned forward, hoping just to catch a glimpse.

To his surprise, Jesus stopped right beneath the tree. He looked up, his eyes meeting Zacchaeus. Then Jesus spoke his name: "Zacchaeus, come down immediately. I must stay at your house today."

The crowd gasped. Why would Jesus choose to visit a man like Zacchaeus, known for dishonesty and greed? People muttered in disapproval, but Zacchaeus quickly climbed down, his heart racing. He welcomed Jesus joyfully into his home.

Inside, something remarkable happened. Zacchaeus stood and declared, "Look, Lord, here and now I give half of my possessions to the poor, and if I have cheated anybody out of anything, I will pay back four times the amount." His words came from a heart changed by encountering Jesus.

Jesus looked at him with compassion and said, "Today salvation has come to this house, because this man, too, is a son of Abraham. For the Son of Man came to seek and to save the lost."

The people in Jericho had only seen Zacchaeus for his past mistakes, but Jesus saw who he could become. That day, Zacchaeus's life turned around. He discovered that true wealth is not found in money but in a relationship with the Savior who knows each of us by name.

- Prayer: Lord, thank You for knowing me by name and loving me as I am.
- Reflecting Question: How does it feel to know Jesus sees you personally?
- Key Verse: "For the Son of Man came to seek and to save the lost." (Luke 19:10)
- Faith in Action: Reach out to someone who feels left out this week.
- Gratitude Prompt: Write one way God has accepted you despite your flaws.

The Last Supper

The streets of Jerusalem were crowded as families prepared for the Passover meal. Among them were Jesus and His disciples. He sent Peter and John ahead with specific instructions: they would meet a man carrying a jar of water, and he would lead them to a large upstairs room already prepared. There they would share the Passover together.

As evening fell, Jesus reclined at the table with the twelve. The candles flickered and the aroma of roasted lamb filled the air. Jesus looked at His disciples and said with deep emotion, "I have eagerly desired to eat this Passover with you before I suffer. For I tell you, I will not eat it again until it finds fulfillment in the kingdom of God."

He took a cup of wine, gave thanks, and passed it among them. "Take this and divide it among you. For I will not drink again from the fruit of the vine until the kingdom of God comes." The disciples exchanged quiet glances, sensing the weight of His words but not fully understanding.

Then Jesus picked up the bread. He broke it into pieces, His hands steady and deliberate. He gave it to His disciples and said, "This is my body given for you. Do this in remembrance of me." They took the bread, humbled by the solemn moment.

After the meal, He lifted the cup once more. "This cup is the new covenant in my blood, which is poured out for you." His voice was steady, yet carried a tone of sacrifice and love that would be remembered for generations. The disciples held the cup, tasting the wine, unaware of how soon His words would become reality.

Around the table, conversation stirred, but Jesus remained focused. He spoke of betrayal, of one among them who would turn against Him. The disciples were shocked, each asking who it might be. Yet even in that tension, Jesus continued to teach them about humility and service, reminding them that greatness in God's kingdom was not about power but about serving others. The meal drew to a close, but its meaning would echo forever. The bread and the cup were no longer just elements of Passover. They became symbols of His sacrifice, reminders of the love that would soon be shown on the cross.

- Prayer: Lord, help me remember Your sacrifice every day and live with gratitude for the love You showed.
- Reflecting Question: What does Jesus' sacrifice at the Last Supper mean to you personally?
- Key Verse: "Do this in remembrance of me." (Luke 22:19)
- Faith in Action: Take a quiet moment this week to thank Jesus for giving His life for you.
- Gratitude Prompt: Write down one blessing that came into your life because of Jesus' sacrifice.

Jesus Prays in Gethsemane

The night was heavy with silence as Jesus led His disciples into a garden called Gethsemane. The olive trees stood like watchmen under the moonlight, their branches swaying in the cool night air. Jesus had just shared His last meal with the twelve, and now His heart was weighed down with what was coming.

He stopped and turned to His friends. "Sit here while I go over there and pray," He said. Taking Peter, James, and John a little farther, His voice trembled as He admitted, "My soul is overwhelmed with sorrow to the point of death. Stay here and keep watch with me."

Leaving them behind, Jesus went a short distance away. He fell to the ground, His face pressed against the earth. The weight of the world's sin pressed heavily upon Him. In a voice filled with anguish He prayed, "My Father, if it is possible, may this cup be taken from me. Yet not as I will, but as You will."

After a time, He rose and returned to His friends, but they were asleep. His heart ached, and He spoke softly, "Couldn't you keep watch with me for one hour? Watch and pray so that you will not fall into temptation. The spirit is willing, but the flesh is weak."

Again He went away, deeper into the shadows, and prayed a second time. "My Father, if it is not possible for this cup to be taken away unless I drink it, may Your will be done." His voice was weary but resolute. When He returned, He found the disciples sleeping once more, their eyes heavy with exhaustion. He left them again and prayed a third time, repeating the same words, surrendering fully to the Father's plan. His sweat fell like drops of blood to the ground, each prayer a battle, each word a surrender.

At last, He rose to His feet. His face bore both sorrow and strength. He returned to His disciples, still sleeping, and spoke with calm resolve: "Are you still sleeping and resting? Look, the hour has come, and the Son of Man is delivered into the hands of sinners. Rise, let us go. Here comes my betrayer."

The garden filled with footsteps and flickering torches as soldiers approached. Jesus stood ready, His heart set on obedience, His prayer now answered in the strength to face what lay ahead.

- Prayer: Lord, give me strength to trust Your will over my own, even when it is difficult.
- Reflecting Question: When is it hardest for you to surrender to God's will?
- Key Verse: "Not as I will, but as you will." (Matthew 26:39)
- Faith in Action: Pray about one decision this week by asking for God's will first.
- Gratitude Prompt: Thank God for hearing your prayers even in hard times.

Peter Denies Jesus

The night was heavy with tension as Jesus was led away from the garden where He had been praying. Soldiers surrounded Him, and His disciples, once bold, scattered in fear. Among them was Peter, who had sworn just hours earlier that he would never abandon his Lord. Yet now he followed from a distance, cautious not to be noticed. The group brought Jesus to the high priest's house. A fire was kindled in the courtyard, and people gathered around it to keep warm. Peter slipped in quietly and sat down among them, trying to blend into the shadows. His eyes darted toward the doorway where Jesus was taken, his heart pounding with confusion and fear.

A servant girl noticed him first. She looked at Peter closely and said, "This man was with Him." Startled, Peter shook his head quickly. "I don't know Him," he insisted, his voice sharper than he intended. He turned his face away, hoping the attention would pass.

Moments later, another person pointed at him. "You are one of them." Peter felt the blood rush to his face. He clenched his jaw and replied firmly, "Man, I am not." His hands trembled as he rubbed them together in the firelight, trying to steady his nerves. The sound of voices, whispers, and the crackle of flames filled the night, but Peter could barely hear anything above the pounding of his heart.

An hour passed. Then another man, certain this time, spoke up. "Surely this fellow was with Him. He is a Galilean." The words pierced Peter like arrows. Cornered and desperate, he cried out, "Man, I don't know what you're talking about!" At that very moment, the rooster crowed.

Peter froze. Across the courtyard, Jesus turned and looked directly at him. That single glance carried no anger, only a deep sorrow that reached into Peter's soul. The memory of his bold promise earlier that night flashed before him. "Even if I have to die with You, I will never disown You." Now the truth lay bare in the flickering firelight. He had denied his Lord three times.

Overcome with grief, Peter stumbled out of the courtyard. The cold night air bit his skin as tears streamed down his face. He wept bitterly, knowing he had failed the one he loved most.

- Prayer: Lord, forgive me when I let fear silence my faith. Help me to stay strong and speak boldly about You.
- Reflecting Question: When have you felt tempted to hide your faith out of fear?
- Key Verse: "The Lord turned and looked straight at Peter. Then Peter remembered the word the Lord had spoken to him." (Luke 22:61)
- Faith in Action: Share your faith openly with one person this week, even if it feels uncomfortable.
- Gratitude Prompt: Thank God for the times He has restored you after you have failed.

The Crucifixion of Jesus

The soldiers led Jesus out of the city to a place called Golgotha, the Place of the Skull. A heavy wooden cross was laid upon His shoulders, and though His body was weary from the beatings and the crown of thorns pressed into His brow, He carried it through the crowded streets. People watched in silence, some mocking, others weeping.

When they reached the hill, the soldiers stretched out His hands and nailed them to the wood. They lifted the cross high, placing it between two criminals. A sign was fastened above His head that read, "Jesus of Nazareth, King of the Jews." The chief priests objected, but Pilate refused to change it.

The soldiers cast lots for His clothes, fulfilling the ancient Scripture that said, "They divided my clothes among them and cast lots for my garment." As the hours passed, the sky grew darker, and Jesus, in His agony, looked down and saw His mother standing near the disciple John. He spoke with tenderness, saying to her, "Woman, here is your son," and to John, "Here is your mother." From that moment, John took her into his home.

The crowd stood by as Jesus struggled for breath. Some shouted insults, daring Him to save Himself if He truly was the Son of God. Yet He remained silent, choosing obedience to the Father's will. One of the criminals beside Him mocked, but the other defended Him, asking Jesus to remember him when He came into His kingdom. Jesus answered, "Truly I tell you, today you will be with me in paradise."

As the darkness deepened, Jesus cried out, "I am thirsty." A sponge soaked in vinegar was lifted to His lips. Then, gathering His strength, He spoke words that echoed through all eternity: "It is finished." With that, He bowed His head and gave up His spirit.

At that moment, the earth shook. The curtain of the temple was torn in two from top to bottom, symbolizing that the way to God was now open through His sacrifice. A centurion who had witnessed everything declared, "Surely this man was the Son of God."

Jesus' body was later taken down and laid in a nearby tomb, but the hill of Golgotha would forever be remembered as the place where the greatest act of love was shown to the world.

- Prayer: Lord, thank You for giving Your life for me. Help me never forget the depth of Your love.
- Reflecting Question: How does Jesus' sacrifice on the cross change the way you see your life?
- Key Verse: "It is finished." (John 19:30)
- Faith in Action: Share with one person this week what the cross means to you personally.
- Gratitude Prompt: Thank God for the gift of salvation and write down two reasons you are thankful for Jesus' sacrifice.

The Resurrection of Jesus

Early on the first day of the week, just as the sun was beginning to rise, Mary Magdalene and the other women walked to the tomb where Jesus had been laid. They carried spices with them, their hearts heavy with grief. They wondered who would roll away the stone from the entrance, for it was large and sealed shut.

When they arrived, the stone was already moved, and the tomb was empty. An angel clothed in dazzling white appeared to them and said, "Do not be afraid. I know you are looking for Jesus, who was crucified. He is not here. He has risen, just as He said."

Fear and joy filled the women at the same time. They ran quickly to tell the disciples, but along the way Jesus Himself appeared before them. They fell at His feet, overwhelmed with awe and relief. He spoke to them gently, "Do not be afraid. Go and tell My brothers to go to Galilee. There they will see Me."

Meanwhile, the disciples were gathered in a locked room, weighed down with sorrow and fear. Suddenly Jesus stood among them and said, "Peace be with you." He showed them His hands and His side, and their fear melted into gladness. He was alive, just as He had promised.

Later, one disciple named Thomas was not present when Jesus first appeared. He doubted the others' words and said he would not believe unless he could see and touch the wounds himself. A week later, Jesus came again into the locked room. He turned to Thomas and said, "Put your finger here. See My hands. Stop doubting and believe." Thomas fell to his knees, declaring, "My Lord and my God!"

In the days that followed, Jesus appeared to many of His followers. He walked with them, ate with them, and spoke to them about the kingdom of God. What had seemed like the darkest defeat became the greatest victory. Death had been conquered, and hope had risen from the grave.

The disciples who once hid in fear were now filled with courage. The empty tomb was not only proof that Jesus was alive but also the foundation of their mission to share the good news with the world. From Jerusalem to the farthest lands, they carried a message that still echoes today: Jesus lives.

- Prayer: Lord, thank You that death is defeated and hope is alive because of Jesus.
- Reflecting Question: What does the resurrection mean for your daily life right now?
- Key Verse: "He is not here; he has risen, just as he said." (Matthew 28:6)
- Faith in Action: Share a message of hope with someone who feels discouraged this week.
- Gratitude Prompt: List three reasons you are thankful for Jesus' resurrection.

The Great Commission

The eleven disciples traveled to Galilee, climbing the familiar slope of a mountain where Jesus had told them to meet Him. The air was heavy with anticipation. These were the same men who had once fled in fear, yet now they gathered with hearts full of questions and hope. As they reached the summit, they saw Jesus standing there, alive and radiant. Some immediately bowed down in worship, while others still wrestled with doubt, unable to grasp the fullness of what had happened.

Jesus stepped closer, His voice calm and steady. He told them that all authority in heaven and on earth had been given to Him. The weight of those words hung in the air, reassuring the uncertain and strengthening the weary. The disciples had witnessed His power over storms, sickness, demons, even death itself. Now He declared that every ounce of that power belonged to Him forever.

Then Jesus gave them a task that would stretch far beyond their imagination. He commanded them to go and make disciples of all nations, not just their own people but every tribe, every language, every corner of the world. They were to baptize in the name of the Father, the Son, and the Holy Spirit. They were to teach others everything He had taught them, passing on His words of life as faithfully as they had received them.

For men who had once been fishermen, tax collectors, and ordinary workers, the assignment seemed overwhelming. Yet Jesus did not leave them with an impossible mission. He ended with a promise, one that would echo in their hearts for the rest of their lives: "I am with you always, to the very end of the age." His presence would go with them into every village, every city, every distant land. Even when they felt weak or unprepared, He would be near, guiding and sustaining them.

As the wind brushed across the hillside, the disciples began to understand that this was not just an ending but a beginning. The story of Jesus was not closing with His resurrection; it was unfolding through them. They would carry His message across seas and deserts, through prisons and palaces, into homes and marketplaces. Wherever they went, they would remember His words on that mountain, spoken with authority and sealed with a promise that could never be broken.

- Prayer: Lord, give me boldness to share Your love with others.
- Reflecting Question: How can you be a witness for Jesus in your daily life?
- Key Verse: "Therefore go and make disciples of all nations..." (Matthew 28:19)
- Faith in Action: Share one Bible verse or encouragement with a friend this week.
- Gratitude Prompt: Thank God for the people who first shared the gospel with you.

The Coming of the Holy Spirit

The city of Jerusalem was crowded with visitors from many nations. Jews from every corner of the known world had gathered to celebrate the Feast of Pentecost. The streets were alive with the sounds of different languages, merchants selling their goods, and families moving toward the temple to worship.

In an upstairs room not far from the temple courts, about 120 followers of Jesus were gathered together. They had been waiting just as Jesus told them before He ascended into heaven. He had promised that the Father would send them power from above, though none of them fully understood what that meant. Still, they prayed, waited, and held on to His words.

On the morning of Pentecost, as they were together in that room, something extraordinary happened. A sound like a powerful wind rushed through the house. It was not a gentle breeze but a roar that filled every corner of the place where they sat. Startled, the disciples looked around at one another, and then they saw it. Flames appeared, small tongues of fire that separated and came to rest on each of them.

In that moment, they were filled with the Holy Spirit. Joy and boldness welled up inside them. Words tumbled out of their mouths, but they were not speaking in their native language. Instead, each of them spoke in languages they had never learned. They rose from their seats and moved outside into the bustling streets, their voices carrying over the noise of the crowd.

People stopped in amazement. Visitors from Mesopotamia, Egypt, Rome, and many other regions stared in wonder. They could hear these Galileans speaking in their own native tongues, declaring the wonders of God. Some were astonished and asked one another what it could mean. Others sneered and accused them of being drunk, though it was still early in the day.

Peter stood with the Eleven and raised his voice above the crowd. No longer afraid as he had been on the night Jesus was arrested, he spoke with conviction. He explained that what they were witnessing was the fulfillment of God's promise through the prophet Joel, that He would pour out His Spirit on all people. Peter told them about Jesus, His death, and His resurrection, and how He had been exalted to the right hand of God. The message pierced the hearts of many who listened. That day, about three thousand people believed, were baptized, and joined the community of believers. What began in an upstairs room with prayer and waiting became the birth of the Church, empowered by the Holy Spirit.

- Prayer: Holy Spirit, fill me with Your power and guide my words.
- Reflecting Question: How can the Holy Spirit help you in your everyday struggles?
- Key Verse: "All of them were filled with the Holy Spirit." (Acts 2:4)
- Faith in Action: Pray before starting something important this week, asking the Spirit's help.
- Gratitude Prompt: Thank God for one way the Spirit has comforted or guided you.

Peter Heals the Beggar

It was the hour of prayer at the temple, and people were streaming through the gates. At the entrance called Beautiful Gate, a man was being carried by his friends. Every day they placed him there, for he had been lame since birth and had no way of walking. From morning until evening, he begged for coins from those entering to worship.

On this day, as Peter and John approached, the man lifted his eyes with a faint hope that they might offer him something. His hands stretched out, waiting for the familiar clink of coins to drop into his palm.

Peter looked straight at him and said, "Look at us." The man fixed his gaze on them, expecting to receive money. But Peter's words were unexpected: "Silver and gold I do not have, but what I do have I give you. In the name of Jesus Christ of Nazareth, walk."

Peter reached out his hand and pulled the man to his feet. In that instant, strength filled his ankles and legs. For the first time in his life, he stood firm. His eyes widened in wonder as he realized he could walk. Not only did he stand, but he began to walk forward, and then he leaped into the air with joy.

The man followed Peter and John into the temple courts, his steps unsteady at first, then confident. He walked, jumped, and praised God aloud so that everyone could hear. Worshippers turned their heads in amazement. Some rubbed their eyes in disbelief, recognizing him as the same man who had sat for years at the gate, begging for spare change.

Whispers spread quickly through the crowd. "Isn't this the lame man who sat by the gate?" "How is he walking now?" The man's joy was unstoppable. He clung to Peter and John, overwhelmed with gratitude and excitement, unable to contain the story of what had happened to him.

All the people were filled with wonder and awe, astonished at the miracle they had witnessed. The temple, a place that had seen countless prayers and rituals, now echoed with the shouts of a man who had been restored by the power of Jesus' name.

- Prayer: Lord, use me to bring hope and encouragement to others.
- Reflecting Question: How can you help someone in need this week?
- Key Verse: "Silver or gold I do not have, but what I do have I give you." (Acts 3:6)
- Faith in Action: Offer practical help or encouragement to someone struggling.
- Gratitude Prompt: Thank God for a time He met your need unexpectedly.

Stephen the First Martyr

Stephen was chosen as one of the seven men to help care for the widows in the early church. He was known for being full of faith and the Holy Spirit, and wherever he went, God worked powerfully through him. People marveled at his wisdom and the way he spoke with boldness about Jesus.

Not everyone was pleased with Stephen's testimony. Some leaders became jealous and angry. They tried to argue with him, but they could not stand against the wisdom and Spirit by which he spoke. Their frustration grew until they secretly persuaded others to accuse him of blasphemy. Stephen was dragged before the council, where false witnesses twisted his words. Yet even in the midst of lies, his face shone like that of an angel.

As the council looked at him, Stephen began to speak. He told the story of Israel, from Abraham to Moses to David, showing how God had guided His people through the centuries. He reminded them of how often the people had resisted God's messengers. Finally, Stephen declared that they were resisting the Holy Spirit just as their ancestors had done. He told them plainly that they had betrayed and killed the Righteous One, Jesus.

The leaders were furious. Their anger burned as they clenched their teeth. But Stephen, full of the Holy Spirit, looked up to heaven. His eyes opened to a vision of God's glory. He saw Jesus standing at the right hand of God, ready to receive him. "Look," Stephen said, "I see heaven open and the Son of Man standing at the right hand of God."

The crowd could not bear to hear it. Covering their ears, they rushed at him as one. They dragged him outside the city and began to stone him. As the heavy stones struck his body, Stephen prayed. His voice rose above the chaos. "Lord Jesus, receive my spirit." Then, with his last breath, he cried out, "Lord, do not hold this sin against them."

And with those words, Stephen fell asleep in the Lord. His courage, his faith, and his forgiveness would never be forgotten. The church mourned deeply, yet his example became a light for all who would one day face trials for their faith.

- Prayer: Lord, give me courage to stand firm in my faith no matter the cost.
- Reflecting Question: What might make you afraid to speak boldly about Jesus?
- Key Verse: "Lord Jesus, receive my spirit." (Acts 7:59)
- Faith in Action: Pray for Christians around the world who face persecution.
- Gratitude Prompt: Thank God for the freedom to worship Him openly.

Saul's Conversion

Saul was known and feared throughout the land. He was a man of determination, relentless in his mission to destroy the followers of Jesus. With authority from the high priest, he set out for Damascus, intent on finding any who belonged to the Way, men or women, to drag them back to Jerusalem in chains.

As he traveled along the dusty road, his companions by his side, the midday sun burned hot above them. Suddenly, a brilliant light flashed from heaven, brighter than the sun, surrounding him with overwhelming force. Saul fell to the ground, shielding his face. A voice called out, clear and commanding, "Saul, Saul, why do you persecute me?"

Shaken, Saul asked, "Who are you, Lord?"

The answer came with power. "I am Jesus, whom you are persecuting. Now get up and go into the city, and you will be told what you must do."

His companions stood speechless, hearing the sound but seeing no one. When Saul opened his eyes, he realized he was blind. Darkness covered his sight. The men traveling with him led him by the hand into Damascus. For three days Saul could not see, and he neither ate nor drank.

In Damascus lived a disciple named Ananias. The Lord spoke to him in a vision: "Go to the house of Judas on Straight Street and ask for a man from Tarsus named Saul. He is praying. I have chosen him as my instrument to proclaim my name to the Gentiles."

Ananias trembled at the thought. Saul's reputation had reached every believer. He had heard of Saul's cruelty and the harm he had caused in Jerusalem. Still, trusting God, he obeyed.

Ananias went to the house and placed his hands on Saul. "Brother Saul, the Lord Jesus, who appeared to you on the road, has sent me so that you may see again and be filled with the Holy Spirit." Immediately something like scales fell from Saul's eyes. His sight was restored, and he looked at Ananias with new clarity. He rose at once and was baptized. Strength returned to his body as he ate and drank, and strength filled his spirit as he began a new life, no longer Saul the persecutor, but Paul the chosen servant of Christ.

- Prayer: Lord, change my heart and use me for Your purpose.
- Reflecting Question: How has God changed you since you first believed?
- Key Verse: "I am Jesus, whom you are persecuting." (Acts 9:5)
- Faith in Action: Share your personal faith story with someone this week.
- Gratitude Prompt: Write one way God has transformed your life.

Peter and Cornelius

Cornelius was a Roman centurion, respected by his soldiers and admired for his fairness. Though he was not Jewish, he believed in the God of Israel. He gave generously to the poor and prayed faithfully, seeking to understand more about the Lord. One afternoon, as Cornelius prayed, an angel appeared before him with a clear message. The angel told him that God had heard his prayers and remembered his kindness. Cornelius was instructed to send men to the city of Joppa to bring back a man named Peter.

Obeying immediately, Cornelius sent three men to find Peter. Meanwhile, in Joppa, Peter went to the rooftop to pray around noon. As he grew hungry, he fell into a vision. He saw heaven open and a large sheet being lowered by its four corners. Inside were animals of every kind, clean and unclean. A voice told Peter, "Get up, Peter. Kill and eat." Peter protested, insisting he had never eaten anything considered impure. But the voice replied, "Do not call anything impure that God has made clean." This happened three times before the vision ended, leaving Peter deeply puzzled.

While Peter was still reflecting on the vision, Cornelius's men arrived at the house where he was staying. The Spirit told Peter to go with them without hesitation. The next day, Peter set out with the men and a few believers from Joppa. When they reached Caesarea, Cornelius was waiting with his family and friends. As Peter entered, Cornelius fell at his feet in reverence, but Peter lifted him up, saying, "Stand up, I am only a man myself."

Inside, Peter found the house full of people eager to hear God's message. Peter began to speak, realizing the meaning of his vision. He said, "I now understand that God does not show favoritism, but accepts everyone who fears Him and does what is right." He shared the good news of Jesus Christ, how He lived, died, and rose again to bring forgiveness of sins.

As Peter spoke, the Holy Spirit came upon all who were listening. The Jewish believers who came with Peter were astonished that the gift of the Spirit was poured out even on Gentiles. Cornelius and his household began praising God and speaking in tongues. Peter then declared that they should be baptized in the name of Jesus Christ. From that day, a new chapter began: the message of Jesus was for all people, not just one nation.

- Prayer: Lord, break down the barriers in my heart and help me see others as You do.
- Reflecting Question: How can you show God's love to someone who is different from you?
- Key Verse: "I now realize how true it is that God does not show favoritism." (Acts 10:34)
- Faith in Action: Reach out to someone outside your usual circle and show them kindness.
- Gratitude Prompt: Thank God for including you in His family, no matter your background.

Paul and Silas in Prison

Paul and Silas were traveling through the city of Philippi when they encountered a slave girl possessed by a spirit that earned her owners a great deal of money. She followed them for days, shouting that they were servants of the Most High God. At last, Paul commanded the spirit to leave her in the name of Jesus, and immediately she was set free.

Her owners were furious, realizing their source of profit was gone. They seized Paul and Silas and dragged them before the city officials. False accusations were hurled against them, and without a fair trial, they were beaten severely and thrown into prison. Their feet were fastened in stocks, and they were left bruised and chained in the inner cell.

The night was long and painful, yet Paul and Silas did not give in to despair. Instead of groaning, they began to pray and sing hymns to God. Their voices rose above the darkness, filling the prison halls. The other prisoners listened in amazement, hearing songs of praise from men who should have been broken. Suddenly, a violent earthquake shook the foundations of the prison. Doors flew open, and everyone's chains fell loose. Freedom was right in front of them, yet Paul and Silas did not flee.

The jailer woke in terror, seeing the doors open. Believing the prisoners had escaped, he prepared to take his own life. But Paul cried out loudly, "Do not harm yourself! We are all here!" Trembling, the jailer called for lights and rushed inside. Falling to his knees before Paul and Silas, he asked, "Sirs, what must I do to be saved?"

They answered, "Believe in the Lord Jesus, and you will be saved—you and your household." That very night, the jailer washed their wounds and brought them into his home. He and his family believed and were baptized with joy. By morning, the magistrates ordered Paul and Silas to be released. They left the prison not as defeated prisoners, but as men whose faith had turned a night of suffering into a testimony of God's power and salvation.

- Prayer: Lord, help me praise You even in difficult times, knowing that You are always in control.
- Reflecting Question: How can worship change your perspective when life feels unfair or heavy?
- Key Verse: "About midnight Paul and Silas were praying and singing hymns to God, and the other prisoners were listening to them." (Acts 16:25)
- Faith in Action: Choose one moment this week to worship or pray when you feel discouraged instead of giving in to negativity.
- Gratitude Prompt: Thank God for a time when He turned a difficult situation into an opportunity for hope.

Paul's Shipwreck

The journey to Rome had begun under uneasy skies. Paul, a prisoner bound for trial, warned the sailors that danger lay ahead if they sailed during this season. His words were brushed aside, and the ship set out across the open sea.

At first the wind seemed gentle, pushing them forward. Soon, however, a violent storm swept down, turning the calm into chaos. The sea roared, waves crashed over the deck, and the ship groaned under the strain. Day after day the tempest raged without mercy. The crew threw cargo overboard to lighten the load, but the storm only grew stronger. Darkness covered the skies, and hope slipped away from the men who trembled on board.

In the midst of fear and despair, Paul stood with courage. He told the sailors and prisoners that an angel of God had appeared to him during the night. The angel declared that Paul would indeed stand trial before Caesar and that every person on the ship would be spared. "Take courage," Paul said. "I believe God, that it will happen just as He told me."

The storm continued for two long weeks. Exhaustion and hunger weighed heavily on everyone. On the fourteenth night, the sailors sensed land was near. They dropped anchors and prayed for daylight. At dawn, Paul urged them to eat, breaking bread and giving thanks to God before all. His faith brought strength to weary hearts.

When daylight came, they spotted a bay with a sandy shore. The crew cut loose the anchors and ran the ship aground. The vessel struck a sandbar, and the waves smashed it until the hull broke apart. Panic set in, but the soldiers allowed everyone to swim or cling to planks. One by one, men tumbled into the sea, clutching fragments of the shattered ship.

Through crashing waves and driving spray, all two hundred and seventy–six souls reached the land. Not one life was lost, just as Paul had said. Cold, wet, and shaken, they stood on the shore of Malta, alive because of God's mercy.

- Prayer: Lord, give me peace and courage when I feel surrounded by storms.
- Reflecting Question: How do you usually respond when life feels out of control?
- Key Verse: "Keep up your courage, because not one of you will be lost." (Acts 27:22)
- Faith in Action: Encourage someone going through a hard time with words of hope.
- Gratitude Prompt: Thank God for protecting you in a difficult situation.

The Armor of God

Paul sat in prison, surrounded by the heavy chains of his confinement. Roman soldiers stood guard, their armor shining in the dim light. Paul had seen many soldiers before, but now he looked more closely at what they wore. Each piece had a purpose, protecting the body and preparing them for battle. As he watched, God gave him an image of what it means to live as a follower of Christ in a world full of challenges and temptations.

The soldier's belt held everything together. Paul thought of truth, the foundation of faith. Just as the belt kept the armor secure, truth held a believer steady against lies. Next came the breastplate, covering the chest and guarding the heart. Paul compared it to righteousness, living in a way that honors God and keeps the heart pure.

Paul's eyes moved to the soldier's sandals. They were made for long marches, strong and firm. He pictured the gospel of peace, giving believers stability and readiness to go wherever God called them. Then he looked at the shield, wide enough to block arrows and protect the whole body. Faith, Paul realized, was like that shield, able to extinguish the flaming arrows of doubt, fear, and temptation.

The helmet was essential for battle, protecting the head and mind. Paul saw salvation as the helmet, guarding the thoughts of every believer and reminding them they belonged to Christ. Finally, the soldier carried a sword, sharp and strong. Paul knew this represented the Word of God, the only weapon powerful enough to defeat the enemy and cut through lies.

As Paul reflected, he wrote to the believers in Ephesus. He told them that life was a battle, not against people, but against spiritual forces of darkness. To stand strong, they needed to put on every piece of God's armor. With truth, righteousness, peace, faith, salvation, and the Word, they would be ready to face whatever came against them. And above all, he urged them to pray at all times, staying connected to God, who was their true strength.

Even from prison, Paul's words carried power and hope. The picture of the Roman soldier became a reminder that every believer could stand firm, fully equipped by God. The armor was not heavy metal but spiritual protection, freely given by the Lord who promised to be with His people in every battle.

- Prayer: Lord, clothe me with Your armor so I can stand strong in faith.
- Reflecting Question: Which part of the armor of God do you need most right now?
- Key Verse: "Put on the full armor of God." (Ephesians 6:11)
- Faith in Action: Memorize one piece of the armor of God and apply it this week.
- Gratitude Prompt: Thank God for giving you spiritual strength to face challenges.

The Fruit of the Spirit

Paul wrote a letter to the believers in Galatia while he was guiding young churches through challenges and confusion. Some people were teaching that faith in Jesus was not enough, that rules and rituals had to be followed in order to be accepted by God. Paul reminded them that life in Christ was not about empty rituals but about transformation through the Holy Spirit.

He explained that when people live only for themselves, their actions show selfishness, anger, jealousy, and division. But when they surrender their hearts to God, the Spirit begins to change them from the inside out. Paul used the image of fruit growing on a healthy tree to describe what life with God looks like.

"The fruit of the Spirit," Paul wrote, "is love, joy, peace, patience, kindness, goodness, faithfulness, gentleness, and self-control." These were not things believers could create on their own. Just as fruit grows naturally from a tree that is rooted in good soil, these qualities grow in a person who stays connected to God.

Paul wanted the Galatians to see that the Spirit's fruit was the true sign of a changed life. Love was more powerful than hatred. Joy could exist even in hardship. Peace came from trusting God's control. Patience, kindness, and goodness showed up in the way believers treated one another. Faithfulness meant staying true even when it was hard. Gentleness revealed strength under control. And self-control gave the power to resist temptations that once seemed impossible.

These fruits were not for personal pride but for blessing others. A tree does not eat its own fruit; it provides nourishment to those around it. In the same way, when the Spirit grows His fruit in a believer's life, others are encouraged, strengthened, and drawn closer to God.

Paul ended his teaching with a challenge. Those who belong to Christ should "keep in step with the Spirit." It was not about rushing ahead or falling behind but walking each day in rhythm with God, letting Him shape their character and their actions.

- Prayer: Holy Spirit, grow Your fruit in my life every day.
- Reflecting Question: Which fruit of the Spirit do you want to grow more in your life?
- Key Verse: "The fruit of the Spirit is love, joy, peace, forbearance, kindness, goodness, faithfulness, gentleness and self-control." (Galatians 5:22–23)
- Faith in Action: Choose one fruit of the Spirit to practice intentionally this week.
- Gratitude Prompt: Thank God for showing one of these fruits in your life recently.

The Greatest Commandment

The city of Jerusalem was crowded with people. Teachers of the law gathered around Jesus, trying to test Him with questions. They wanted to trap Him with His own words and prove that He was not who He claimed to be.

One of them, an expert in the law, stepped forward with a serious expression. He asked, "Teacher, which is the greatest commandment in the Law?" Around them, the crowd grew silent. Everyone waited for Jesus' reply, knowing this was not an easy question. The law contained hundreds of commandments, and no one could agree on which was most important.

Jesus looked at the man and answered with calm authority. "Love the Lord your God with all your heart and with all your soul and with all your mind. This is the first and greatest commandment." The words echoed through the crowd. People nodded, recognizing these words from the Scriptures they had known since childhood.

But Jesus did not stop there. He continued, "And the second is like it: Love your neighbor as yourself. All the Law and the Prophets hang on these two commandments."

The people exchanged glances, surprised by His answer. The law was vast and detailed, yet Jesus had summarized it into two clear instructions. Love God completely. Love others sincerely. Everything else rested on these truths.

The teacher who had asked the question had no argument left. He could not trap Jesus, because His answer revealed the very heart of God's law. Instead of focusing on rules, Jesus reminded them that the foundation of faith is love.

As the crowd slowly dispersed, His words remained. To love God with everything and to love others as ourselves was more powerful than rituals, sacrifices, or empty traditions. It was the commandment that brought life, purpose, and true relationship with God and with people.

- Prayer: Lord, help me to love You above all and love others sincerely.
- Reflecting Question: What's one way you can show love to God and others today?
- Key Verse: "Love the Lord your God with all your heart and with all your soul and with all your mind." (Matthew 22:37)
- Faith in Action: Do one act of love for someone without expecting anything back.
- Gratitude Prompt: Thank God for someone who has shown you true love.

The Widow's Offering

The temple courtyard was filled with the sound of footsteps, voices, and the clinking of coins as people came forward to give their offerings. Some of the wealthy approached proudly, carrying heavy purses. They poured large amounts into the collection boxes, their coins ringing loudly as they fell. Others watched with admiration, impressed by the grand displays of generosity.

Near the back of the crowd stood a widow, her figure small and her clothing worn. She clutched a small cloth pouch in her hand. Inside were two tiny copper coins, the smallest coins in circulation. They were all she had left, but in her heart, she knew they belonged to God.

She moved quietly toward the offering boxes. The wealthy givers hardly noticed her as she slipped between them. Her hands trembled slightly as she dropped the coins into the box. The sound was barely audible compared to the heavy coins of the rich, but it was the sound of her faith. She turned to leave, unnoticed by most, but seen by the One who mattered.

Jesus sat nearby with his disciples, watching as people came forward with their gifts. He saw the proud faces of the rich as they gave out of their abundance. But when the widow placed her two coins into the box, his eyes lit up with admiration.

Calling his disciples to him, Jesus said, "Truly I tell you, this poor widow has put more into the treasury than all the others. They gave out of their wealth, but she, out of her poverty, gave everything she had to live on."

The disciples looked at one another in silence. They had seen the rich make grand offerings, yet Jesus honored the smallest gift of all. The widow had not given leftovers. She had given her heart.

Though her gift seemed insignificant to others, in God's eyes it was priceless. Her two coins still echo through history as a reminder that the value of an offering is not measured by its size, but by the faith and love behind it.

- Prayer: Lord, teach me to give generously from the heart, no matter how small the gift.
- Reflecting Question: How can you give to God and others with sincerity rather than show?
- Key Verse: "This poor widow has put more into the treasury than all the others." (Mark 12:43)
- Faith in Action: Share your time, talent, or resources with someone in need this week, no matter the amount.
- Gratitude Prompt: Thank God for what you already have and for the chance to give, even in small ways.

The Parable of the Talents

Jesus told a story about a man who was preparing to go on a long journey. Before he left, he called his servants and entrusted his wealth to them. To one he gave five talents of gold, to another two, and to the last one he gave a single talent, each according to their ability. Then the man went away.

The servant who had received five talents went to work at once. He traded and invested until his master's money doubled. In the same way, the servant with two talents worked hard and gained two more. But the servant who had received only one talent was afraid. Instead of using what he had been given, he dug a hole in the ground and hid his master's money.

After a long time, the master returned and called his servants to settle accounts. The man who had received five talents stepped forward and presented ten. "Master," he said, "you trusted me with five talents. See, I have gained five more." The master smiled and replied, "Well done, good and faithful servant. You have been faithful with a few things; I will put you in charge of many. Come and share in your master's happiness."

Then the man with two talents came forward. "Master, you entrusted me with two talents. I have gained two more." The master gave him the same praise. "Well done, good and faithful servant. Come and share in your master's happiness."

Finally the man who had received one talent came. His voice trembled as he said, "Master, I knew you were a hard man, harvesting where you have not sown. I was afraid and went out and hid your talent in the ground. See, here is what belongs to you."

The master frowned. "You wicked, lazy servant. You knew I harvest where I have not sown? Then you should have at least put my money on deposit with the bankers, so that I would have received it back with interest." He took the talent from him and gave it to the servant with ten. Then he said, "For whoever has will be given more, and they will have an abundance. Whoever does not have, even what they have will be taken from them."

- Prayer: Lord, help me use my gifts to honor You and bless others.
- Reflecting Question: What talent or gift has God given you to grow?
- Key Verse: "Well done, good and faithful servant." (Matthew 25:23)
- Faith in Action: Use one of your skills this week to serve someone.
- Gratitude Prompt: Thank God for a specific gift or talent you have.

The Parable of the Lost Sheep

The crowds often gathered around Jesus, eager to hear his words. Many of them were tax collectors and people considered sinners by the religious leaders. The Pharisees and teachers of the law grumbled, whispering among themselves that Jesus welcomed sinners and even ate with them.

Jesus, knowing their hearts, decided to tell them a story. He wanted them to understand the depth of God's love, a love that reaches even to the ones who wander away.

"Suppose one of you has a hundred sheep," Jesus began, his voice carrying over the crowd. "If one of them gets lost, what will you do? Will you not leave the ninety-nine in the open field and go after the one that wandered off until you find it?"

The people leaned in, picturing the image. A shepherd counting his flock and realizing one small sheep was missing. The shepherd would not shrug his shoulders and let it go. He would climb the hills, search through the valleys, and call out into the night until his voice grew hoarse. He would not stop until the sheep was found.

"And when he finds it," Jesus continued, "he joyfully puts it on his shoulders and carries it home. Then he calls his friends and neighbors together and says, 'Rejoice with me. I have found my lost sheep.'"

The image stirred something in the listeners. A shepherd rejoicing over one sheep. Friends and neighbors gathering to celebrate. The crowd understood the joy of finding what was lost, and yet this joy was greater, deeper, more eternal.

"I tell you," Jesus said, looking directly at the Pharisees, "in the same way there will be more rejoicing in heaven over one sinner who repents than over ninety-nine righteous persons who do not need to repent."

The story ended, but the meaning hung heavy in the air. For those who felt unworthy, it was a message of hope: God would not abandon them. For those who thought themselves righteous, it was a reminder that God's heart longs for the lost to return.

The people listened, some with tears in their eyes. They realized that God's love was not distant or cold. It was personal, pursuing, relentless. A shepherd who would leave the ninety-nine to search for one.

- Prayer: Lord, thank You for seeking me when I wander away and carrying me back to safety.
- Reflecting Question: How do you respond when someone you know feels left out or lost?
- Key Verse: "Rejoice with me; I have found my lost sheep." (Luke 15:6)
- Faith in Action: Reach out to someone who seems lonely this week and remind them they matter.
- Gratitude Prompt: Write one way God has brought you back when you strayed.

The Parable of the Sower

A large crowd gathered along the shore as Jesus stepped into a boat and began to teach. The people leaned forward, eager to hear every word. His voice carried across the water as He told them a story.

"A farmer went out to sow his seed," Jesus began. "As he scattered the seed, some fell along the path. The birds swooped down quickly and ate it up. Other seed fell on rocky places, where there was not much soil. It sprang up quickly, but when the sun rose, the plants were scorched. They had no root, and they withered away. Still other seed fell among thorns. The thorns grew up and choked the plants, and they bore no grain. But some seed fell on good soil. It grew, it multiplied, and produced a harvest, thirty, sixty, even a hundred times what was sown."

The people exchanged curious looks, wondering at the meaning of His words. Some nodded, others whispered to one another, trying to understand. Jesus raised His voice and finished with a challenge. "Whoever has ears to hear, let them hear."

Later, when the crowd had left, His disciples asked Him about the parable. Jesus explained it with patience. "The seed is the word of God. The seed along the path is like those who hear the word, but Satan comes and takes it away before it can take root. The seed on rocky ground is like those who hear the word and receive it with joy, but they have no root. When trouble or persecution comes, they quickly fall away. The seed among thorns is like those who hear the word but allow worries, wealth, and pleasures to choke it, making it unfruitful. But the seed on good soil is like those who hear the word, accept it, and bear fruit, thirty, sixty, or a hundredfold."

The disciples listened carefully, their hearts stirred. They began to understand that the condition of the soil was not about fields of earth, but about the soil of the heart. Jesus looked at them with steady eyes, as if inviting them to consider what kind of soil they would be.

- Prayer: Lord, prepare my heart to receive and live out Your Word.
- Reflecting Question: Which type of "soil" best represents your heart right now?
- Key Verse: "Others, like seed sown on good soil, hear the word, accept it, and produce a crop." (Mark 4:20)
- Faith in Action: Set aside time to reflect on a Bible verse and apply it this week.
- Gratitude Prompt: Thank God for one truth from His Word that has changed you.

The Parable of the Mustard Seed

Jesus often spoke to the crowds in parables, simple stories with deep meaning. One day, as people gathered around Him near the lakeshore, He looked at them and began to tell a story about something very small.

"The kingdom of heaven is like a mustard seed," He said. The people knew what a mustard seed looked like. It was one of the tiniest seeds they could imagine, so small it could rest on the tip of a finger. Farmers scattered them in the fields, and they seemed almost insignificant compared to the larger seeds of wheat or barley.

But Jesus reminded them that even a seed so small could surprise everyone. When planted in the ground, the mustard seed grew quickly. It pushed through the soil and stretched toward the sky, reaching a height much greater than anyone would expect from such a tiny beginning. In time, it became a tree-like plant, with wide branches spreading out in all directions. Birds flew down and found shelter in its shade, building nests among the branches and resting in its protection.

The people listening could picture it clearly. They had seen these little seeds turn into plants tall enough to tower over them. What seemed insignificant at first became something strong and lasting.

Jesus left them with that image. The kingdom of God, He said, may appear to start small, like a tiny seed. It might look weak or hidden at the beginning. But in time it would grow far beyond what anyone expected. What started with only a few followers would one day spread across the world, offering shelter, hope, and life to all who came to it.

The crowd grew quiet, each person holding the picture in their mind of a small seed becoming something great. Jesus gave no long explanation. His words stayed with them, simple yet powerful, like the seed itself—something small that would keep growing inside their hearts.

- Prayer: Lord, grow my small faith into something strong and lasting.
- Reflecting Question: What small act of faith can you take this week?
- Key Verse: "Though it is the smallest of all seeds, yet when it grows, it is the largest of garden plants." (Matthew 13:32)
- Faith in Action: Take one small step of faith you have been avoiding.
- Gratitude Prompt: Write one way God has grown something small into something big in your life.

The Parable of the Wise and Foolish Builders

Jesus often spoke in parables so that people could understand deep truths through simple images. One day, as He taught the crowds, He told them a story about two men who each decided to build a house. The first man was wise. He carefully chose the spot where his house would stand. He found solid rock as the foundation, steady and unmoving. It was not the easiest place to build. The work was harder, and it took longer to dig into the rock and prepare it. But he knew that if the foundation was strong, the house would stand firm.

The other man was foolish. He chose an easier spot on soft ground, where the sand was smooth and the building went up quickly. His house looked just as fine on the outside as the wise man's. From a distance, both houses might have appeared strong, safe, and ready to last.

Time passed, and both men lived comfortably in their homes. Then the weather changed. Dark clouds gathered, and heavy rain began to fall. The wind howled and beat against the walls. Floodwaters rose, swirling around the foundations of each house.

The storm tested the strength of what each man had built. The wise man's house stood firm. The rain pounded the roof, the rivers surged around it, but it did not move, because it was anchored on solid rock. He stayed safe inside, sheltered from the storm.

But the foolish man's house shook with every gust of wind. The sand beneath it began to shift. The water eroded the foundation, washing it away bit by bit. Soon the walls leaned, the structure cracked, and in one great crash, the house collapsed completely. Nothing was left but ruins, and the man who had built on sand was left with nothing.

When Jesus finished the parable, the meaning was clear. The wise builder was like the person who hears His words and puts them into practice. Their life, built on obedience to God's truth, will remain steady no matter the storms. The foolish builder was like the one who listens but does not act. They may look strong for a while, but when trouble comes, they fall.

- Prayer: Lord, help me build my life on the solid foundation of Your Word.
- Reflecting Question: What does building your life on Jesus look like for you right now?
- Key Verse: "The rain came down, the streams rose, and the winds blew and beat against that house; yet it did not fall, because it had its foundation on the rock." (Matthew 7:25)
- Faith in Action: Identify one habit that helps you build on Jesus and practice it this week.
- Gratitude Prompt: Thank God for being your unshakable foundation in life.

The Parable of the Unforgiving Servant

Peter once came to Jesus with a question. "Lord, how many times shall I forgive my brother or sister who sins against me? Up to seven times?"

Jesus answered, "I tell you, not seven times, but seventy-seven times." Then He told a story to explain what He meant.

There was a king who wanted to settle accounts with his servants. One servant was brought to him who owed him an enormous debt, more than he could ever repay. Since the man could not pay, the king ordered that he and his family be sold to repay what was owed.

The servant fell on his knees before the king. "Be patient with me," he begged, "and I will pay back everything." The king took pity on him, canceled the debt, and let him go free.

But when that servant went out, he found one of his fellow servants who owed him a small amount of money. He grabbed him and began to choke him. "Pay back what you owe me!" he demanded.

The fellow servant fell to his knees and begged him, "Be patient with me, and I will pay it back." But the man refused. Instead, he had his fellow servant thrown into prison until he could pay the debt.

When the other servants saw what had happened, they were greatly distressed and went to tell the king everything that had taken place.

The king called the first servant in. "You wicked servant," he said. "I canceled all that debt of yours because you begged me to. Shouldn't you have had mercy on your fellow servant just as I had on you?"

In anger, the king handed him over to the jailers to be punished until he could pay back all he owed.

Jesus finished by saying, "This is how my heavenly Father will treat each of you unless you forgive your brother or sister from your heart."

- Prayer: Lord, teach me to forgive others as You have forgiven me.
- Reflecting Question: Is there someone you need to forgive right now?
- Key Verse: "Shouldn't you have had mercy on your fellow servant just as I had on you?" (Matthew 18:33)
- Faith in Action: Choose one person to forgive this week, even in a small way.
- Gratitude Prompt: Thank God for His forgiveness in your life.

The Parable of the Ten Virgins

Ten young women once gathered to wait for a wedding celebration. Each of them carried a lamp to light the way when the bridegroom arrived. They were excited, dressed in their best clothes, and ready to join the joyful procession that would lead to the feast.

Five of the women were wise. They brought extra oil along with their lamps, knowing the wait could be long. The other five were foolish. They carried lamps, but no extra oil. To them, it seemed unnecessary. As the hours passed, the bridegroom delayed. The night grew darker and the women grew tired. Eventually, they all fell asleep, lamps flickering beside them.

At midnight, a cry rang out. "Here's the bridegroom! Come out to meet him!" The women jumped up, hearts racing. They trimmed their lamps to shine brightly. The wise women poured their extra oil into the lamps, and their flames burned steady and strong.

But the foolish ones discovered their lamps sputtering out. They turned in panic to the wise women. "Give us some of your oil. Our lamps are going out!"

The wise women shook their heads. "There may not be enough for both us and you. Go quickly to those who sell oil and buy some for yourselves."

The five foolish women hurried away into the night to find oil. While they were gone, the bridegroom arrived. The five wise women, their lamps glowing brightly, joined the procession and entered the feast. The doors closed behind them, shutting out the darkness.

Later, the foolish women returned with oil. They rushed to the door, pounding and calling, "Lord, Lord, open the door for us!" But the bridegroom answered from within, "Truly I tell you, I don't know you."

The wedding continued with music, joy, and laughter, but the foolish women were left outside, regret heavy in their hearts. They had been invited to the celebration, but they had not been ready when the moment came.

- Prayer: Lord, help me to stay prepared and faithful so I am always ready for You.
- Reflecting Question: What does being prepared for Jesus look like in your daily life?
- Key Verse: "Therefore keep watch, because you do not know the day or the hour." (Matthew 25:13)
- Faith in Action: Set aside time this week to strengthen your faith through prayer or Scripture reading.
- Gratitude Prompt: Thank God for giving you time and grace to prepare your heart for Him.

The Parable of the Sheep and the Goats

When Jesus taught His disciples about the coming judgment, He used a powerful picture. He spoke of Himself as the Son of Man, returning in glory and sitting on His throne. All nations would be gathered before Him, and He would separate the people like a shepherd separates the sheep from the goats.

The sheep were placed on His right. These were the ones who had lived with compassion and mercy. Jesus said to them, "Come, you who are blessed by my Father. Take your inheritance, the kingdom prepared for you since the creation of the world."

The sheep were surprised. They asked, "Lord, when did we see You hungry and feed You, or thirsty and give You something to drink? When did we see You a stranger and invite You in, or needing clothes and clothe You? When did we see You sick or in prison and go to visit You?"

The King answered, "Truly I tell you, whatever you did for one of the least of these brothers and sisters of mine, you did for Me."

Then Jesus turned to the goats on His left. These were the ones who had ignored the needs of others and lived only for themselves. He said, "Depart from Me, you who are cursed, into the eternal fire prepared for the devil and his angels."

The goats, shocked, asked, "Lord, when did we see You hungry or thirsty or a stranger or needing clothes or sick or in prison, and did not help You?"

He replied, "Truly I tell you, whatever you did not do for one of the least of these, you did not do for Me."

The sheep went away to eternal life with God, while the goats faced eternal separation. Through this story, Jesus showed His disciples that serving others is the same as serving Him. Acts of kindness, compassion, and care toward those in need are not small or forgotten. They are noticed by God Himself, and they matter for eternity.

- Prayer: Lord, open my eyes to see You in the people who need help around me. Give me compassion to serve with love.
- Reflecting Question: How can you serve someone in need this week as if you were serving Jesus directly?
- Key Verse: "Whatever you did for one of the least of these brothers and sisters of mine, you did for me." (Matthew 25:40)
- Faith in Action: Do something practical this week for someone who has a need, whether big or small.
- Gratitude Prompt: Thank God for opportunities to make a difference in the lives of others.

The Road to Emmaus

Two men were walking along the dusty road that led from Jerusalem to a small village called Emmaus. The sun was beginning to sink, and the weight of recent events pressed heavily on their shoulders. They had been followers of Jesus, full of hope that He was the one who would redeem Israel. But just days before, He had been crucified, and their dreams seemed shattered.

As they walked, they talked about everything that had happened. Confusion and grief filled their words. Suddenly, a stranger joined them. He fell into step beside them and asked, "What are you discussing as you walk along?"

The two men stopped, their faces downcast. "Are you the only one visiting Jerusalem who does not know the things that have happened there in these days?" one of them asked. They explained how Jesus of Nazareth had been a prophet, powerful in word and deed, and how they had hoped He was the Messiah. They told him of the empty tomb and the strange report of angels saying He was alive, yet they could not bring themselves to believe.

The stranger listened and then began to speak. He explained how all the Scriptures pointed to the Messiah, how suffering was part of God's plan before glory would come. As He spoke, the men felt something stirring deep inside them, though they did not understand it fully.

When they reached the village, the men urged Him strongly, "Stay with us, for it is nearly evening; the day is almost over." The stranger accepted and sat down with them at the table. He took bread, gave thanks, broke it, and began to give it to them. In that moment their eyes were opened, and they recognized Him. It was Jesus.

Just as suddenly, He disappeared from their sight. The two men looked at each other in awe. "Were not our hearts burning within us while He talked with us on the road and opened the Scriptures to us?" Without hesitation, they rose and hurried back to Jerusalem, even though night had fallen. They could not keep the news to themselves. They found the other disciples and proclaimed with joy, "It is true! The Lord has risen and has appeared to us!"

- Prayer: Lord, open my eyes to recognize Your presence in my life.
- Reflecting Question: When have you felt God was near even if you did not notice at first?
- Key Verse: "Were not our hearts burning within us while he talked with us on the road?" (Luke 24:32)
- Faith in Action: Take a walk this week and talk to God as if He is walking with you.
- Gratitude Prompt: Thank God for a time He brought hope when you felt discouraged.

The Ascension of Jesus

The disciples gathered together on the Mount of Olives, just outside Jerusalem. The air was filled with both excitement and uncertainty. They had seen Jesus alive after the crucifixion, had listened to His words, and had witnessed the marks in His hands and feet. Now, as they stood with Him, they could not help but wonder what would happen next.

"Lord, are You at this time going to restore the kingdom to Israel?" one of them asked. The question carried the weight of generations longing for freedom and hope.

Jesus looked at them with steady eyes. "It is not for you to know the times or dates the Father has set by His own authority. But you will receive power when the Holy Spirit comes upon you, and you will be My witnesses in Jerusalem, and in all Judea and Samaria, and to the ends of the earth."

The disciples listened carefully. His words were not about earthly power but about a mission far greater than they had imagined. He was entrusting them with the message of salvation, to be carried across the entire world.

As He finished speaking, something extraordinary began to happen. Before their eyes, Jesus was lifted up from the ground. Slowly, He rose higher and higher until a cloud came and hid Him from their sight. The disciples stood in silence, gazing upward, unable to move, their hearts filled with awe.

While they were still looking into the sky, two men dressed in white suddenly appeared beside them. "Men of Galilee," they said, "why do you stand here looking into the sky? This same Jesus, who has been taken from you into heaven, will come back in the same way you have seen Him go."

The disciples lowered their eyes from the heavens. Though Jesus was no longer standing among them, His promise remained. The Holy Spirit would come, and their mission was clear. With a renewed sense of purpose, they turned back toward Jerusalem, ready to wait, to pray, and to begin the work He had given them.

- Prayer: Lord, help me live with hope, knowing You will return one day.
- Reflecting Question: How does the promise of Jesus' return affect your daily life?
- Key Verse: "This same Jesus… will come back in the same way you have seen him go." (Acts 1:11)
- Faith in Action: Share the hope of Jesus' return with someone who feels hopeless.
- Gratitude Prompt: Thank God for the promise of eternal life.

Philip and the Ethiopian

Philip was traveling along the road from Jerusalem to Gaza when an angel of the Lord spoke to him. He was told to go to that desert road, and without hesitation he obeyed. As he walked, he noticed a chariot moving slowly ahead. Inside sat an Ethiopian official, a man of great importance who worked for the queen of Ethiopia. He had been to Jerusalem to worship and was now returning home, reading aloud from the prophet Isaiah.

The Spirit told Philip to go near the chariot. As Philip ran up, he heard the man reading. The words were from Isaiah, speaking about a servant who would suffer and be humiliated. Philip asked gently, "Do you understand what you are reading?"

The Ethiopian looked up and replied, "How can I, unless someone explains it to me?" He invited Philip to climb into the chariot and sit beside him.

The passage the man was reading said, *"He was led like a sheep to the slaughter, and as a lamb before its shearer is silent, so he did not open his mouth."* The Ethiopian turned to Philip and asked, "Tell me, please, who is the prophet talking about, himself or someone else?"

Philip began to explain. Starting with that very passage of Scripture, he told him the good news about Jesus. He spoke of how Jesus fulfilled the prophecy, how He suffered, died, and rose again so that all people could be saved. The Ethiopian listened with an open heart, eager to understand.

As the chariot continued along the road, they came to some water. The Ethiopian's eyes lit up. "Look, here is water. What can stand in the way of my being baptized?" He ordered the chariot to stop, and both he and Philip went down into the water. There Philip baptized him, and the man came up rejoicing.

When they stepped out of the water, the Spirit of the Lord suddenly took Philip away. The Ethiopian did not see him again, but he went on his way filled with joy. Meanwhile, Philip found himself in another town and continued preaching the good news wherever he traveled.

- Prayer: Lord, help me be ready to share my faith with others.
- Reflecting Question: How can you be more prepared to explain what you believe?
- Key Verse: "Then both Philip and the eunuch went down into the water and Philip baptized him." (Acts 8:38)
- Faith in Action: Share a Bible verse with someone this week.
- Gratitude Prompt: Thank God for the people who explained His Word to you.

Ananias and Sapphira

In the early days of the church, the believers were united. They shared everything they had, and no one was in need. Many who owned land or houses sold them and brought the money to the apostles to distribute. The generosity was so great that everyone was cared for, and the church grew strong.

Among the believers was a man named Ananias and his wife, Sapphira. They sold a piece of property, but instead of bringing all the money to the apostles, they secretly held back part of it. They agreed together to pretend they were giving the full amount, hoping to gain the admiration of others without making the full sacrifice.

Ananias came first to the apostles, carrying the portion he had decided to give. He laid it at Peter's feet as though it were the whole amount. But Peter, filled with the Holy Spirit, looked at him and said, "Ananias, why has Satan filled your heart to lie to the Holy Spirit and keep back part of the money? The land was yours to keep or sell. The money was yours to give or not to give. Why pretend? You have not lied to men but to God."

At those words, Ananias fell to the ground and died. Fear swept through everyone who heard about it. The young men wrapped up his body, carried him out, and buried him.

About three hours later, Sapphira came in, not knowing what had happened. Peter asked her, "Tell me, is this the price you and Ananias received for the land?"

"Yes," she answered, "that is the price."

Peter said, "How could you agree to test the Spirit of the Lord? The men who buried your husband are at the door, and they will carry you out also." At that moment, she fell down dead at his feet. The young men came in, found her, and carried her out to be buried beside her husband.

Great fear seized the whole church and all who heard about these events. The story of Ananias and Sapphira became a solemn reminder that honesty before God cannot be faked.

- Prayer: Lord, help me live honestly with You and others.
- Reflecting Question: Why is honesty important in your relationship with God?
- Key Verse: "You have not lied just to human beings but to God." (Acts 5:4)
- Faith in Action: Be completely honest in one area of your life this week.
- Gratitude Prompt: Thank God for forgiving your mistakes and giving second chances.

Barnabas the Encourager

Barnabas was a man whose very name meant "son of encouragement." He was part of the early church in Jerusalem, a community that was growing quickly after Jesus' resurrection. Many believers shared their possessions so that no one would be in need. Barnabas, moved by generosity, sold a field he owned and brought the money to the apostles. His act of selflessness set an example of what it meant to give with a willing heart.

Later, when Saul, who had once persecuted Christians, came to Jerusalem after his dramatic conversion, many believers were afraid of him. They could not believe that the man who had hunted them now claimed to follow Jesus. It was Barnabas who stepped forward. He brought Saul to the apostles, told them of his encounter with the Lord on the road to Damascus, and explained how boldly Saul had preached in the name of Jesus. Because of Barnabas, the church accepted Saul and gave him the chance to serve.

Years passed, and the church in Antioch began to flourish. News of this reached Jerusalem, and the apostles decided to send Barnabas to encourage the new believers. When he arrived, he saw the grace of God at work and was filled with joy. True to his nature, he urged them all to remain faithful to the Lord with steadfast hearts. The church grew stronger because Barnabas believed in them.

Knowing the need for more teachers, Barnabas traveled to Tarsus to find Saul. He brought him back to Antioch, and together they taught large numbers of people. The partnership between Barnabas and Saul became a powerful force for spreading the gospel. Later, when the church began its missionary journeys, Barnabas was chosen alongside Saul to carry the message of Jesus to new lands.

Barnabas is remembered not for great speeches or dramatic miracles, but for his steady encouragement, his generosity, and his ability to see potential in others when no one else did. He helped shape the early church by lifting others up and pointing them to God's faithfulness.

- Prayer: Lord, make me an encourager like Barnabas, quick to see the good in others and to lift them up in faith.
- Reflecting Question: Who in your life needs encouragement right now?
- Key Verse: "He was a good man, full of the Holy Spirit and faith." (Acts 11:24)
- Faith in Action: Encourage one person this week with words or actions.
- Gratitude Prompt: Write down one person who has encouraged you and why.

Paul Preaches in Athens

Paul arrived in Athens, a city full of wisdom, debate, and endless idols. As he walked through the streets, he noticed altars and statues dedicated to many gods. One altar caught his eye. Its inscription read: "To the Unknown God." The people worshiped what they did not understand, and Paul's spirit was stirred within him.

He was invited to the Areopagus, a gathering place where philosophers and citizens met to discuss new ideas. They were curious about this stranger and his teaching about Jesus and the resurrection. With confidence, Paul stood before them and began to speak.

"Men of Athens, I see that in every way you are very religious. As I walked around and looked carefully at your objects of worship, I even found an altar with this inscription: To the Unknown God. You are ignorant of the very thing you worship, and this is what I am going to proclaim to you."

The crowd leaned in as Paul explained that the God who made the world and everything in it does not live in temples built by human hands. He is not served by human effort, because He Himself gives life and breath to all. Paul told them that God created every nation and placed them in their appointed times and places so that people would seek Him and find Him.

Then Paul quoted words familiar to them. "In Him we live and move and have our being. As some of your own poets have said, 'We are His offspring.'" His words connected their culture with the truth of God.

Paul continued boldly. "Since we are God's offspring, we should not think that the divine being is like gold or silver or stone, shaped by human design. In the past, God overlooked such ignorance, but now He commands all people everywhere to repent. For He has set a day when He will judge the world with justice by the man He has appointed. He has given proof of this by raising Him from the dead."

Some sneered when they heard about the resurrection, but others wanted to hear more. A few believed and followed Paul, including Dionysius, a member of the council, and a woman named Damaris. In the heart of Athens, among statues and debates, the truth of the living God was proclaimed.

- Prayer: Lord, help me share my faith in a way others can understand.
- Reflecting Question: How can you explain your faith to someone who doesn't believe?
- Key Verse: "In him we live and move and have our being." (Acts 17:28)
- Faith in Action: Share something about God in a natural conversation this week.
- Gratitude Prompt: Thank God for making Himself known to you.

Paul Writes to the Philippians

Paul sat in a Roman prison, the cold stone walls around him offering little comfort. Chains bound his hands, and yet his spirit remained free. Despite the harshness of his surroundings, his thoughts turned to the believers in Philippi, a community that had supported him from the very beginning of his ministry. He remembered their generosity, their prayers, and their unwavering faith.

Taking up his pen, Paul began to write. His words carried not despair but joy. "Rejoice in the Lord always," he told them, a message that must have seemed strange coming from a man in chains. But Paul's joy was not tied to circumstances. It flowed from knowing Christ and trusting His presence in every situation.

He urged the Philippians to stand firm, to be united, and to live with gentleness. He reminded them that the Lord was near, closer than they might realize. Then Paul addressed one of the greatest struggles every believer faces: worry. "Do not be anxious about anything," he wrote, encouraging them to bring every concern to God in prayer. He assured them that the peace of God, which surpasses all understanding, would guard their hearts and minds in Christ Jesus.

Paul knew what it meant to live with little and what it meant to live with plenty. Through it all, he had discovered the secret of contentment. Whether hungry or well fed, in need or in abundance, he had learned to rely on Christ's strength. "I can do all this through him who gives me strength," he wrote, not as a boast but as a testimony of God's sustaining power.

He also expressed deep gratitude for their gifts and support. Though he did not seek material reward, he rejoiced in their partnership. Their generosity was like a fragrant offering, pleasing to God. Paul assured them that the same God who had provided for him would also supply all their needs according to His riches in glory.

The letter closed with a blessing, as Paul prayed that the grace of the Lord Jesus Christ would be with their spirit. Even in chains, his words carried freedom, hope, and encouragement, echoing across centuries to remind believers that joy and peace are found in Christ alone.

- Prayer: Lord, fill my heart with joy and peace that come only from You.
- Reflecting Question: What worries can you give to God in prayer right now?
- Key Verse: "Do not be anxious about anything... the peace of God... will guard your hearts." (Philippians 4:6–7)
- Faith in Action: Write down one worry and pray over it daily this week.
- Gratitude Prompt: Thank God for one time He replaced your anxiety with peace.

Paul's Teaching on Love

Paul wrote many letters to the early churches, but his words to the Corinthians about love became some of the most famous in all of Scripture. The church in Corinth struggled with division, pride, and arguments about who was the most important. Some valued speaking in tongues, others prized wisdom or knowledge, and many boasted about their spiritual gifts. Paul reminded them that none of these things mattered without love.

He explained that someone could speak every language on earth and even the language of angels, but without love, their words were just noise like a clashing cymbal. A person could have faith strong enough to move mountains, but without love, it was worthless. Even giving away everything to the poor or sacrificing one's life meant nothing if love was not the reason behind it.

Paul then described what real love looks like. Love is patient and kind. It is not jealous or proud. Love does not dishonor others, and it is not selfish or easily angered. It keeps no record of wrongs. Love does not delight in evil but rejoices with the truth. Love always protects, always trusts, always hopes, and always perseveres.

He reminded them that gifts like prophecy, tongues, and knowledge would one day pass away. They were important, but temporary. Love, however, never ends. On this side of life, people know only in part, like looking into a mirror dimly. But one day, they will see clearly, face to face with God. In that moment, all the partial things will fade, but love will remain.

Paul closed this section with a simple but powerful truth. Three great qualities will last forever: faith, hope, and love. Yet the greatest of these is love. He wanted the Corinthians to understand that love was not just a feeling but a way of life, the most important mark of following Jesus.

- Prayer: Lord, teach me to love others the way You love me.
- Reflecting Question: Which quality of love in 1 Corinthians 13 do you need most in your life right now?
- Key Verse: "And now these three remain: faith, hope and love. But the greatest of these is love." (1 Corinthians 13:13)
- Faith in Action: Practice one act of patient, selfless love this week toward someone close to you.
- Gratitude Prompt: Thank God for one person who has shown you unconditional love.

Paul's Race of Faith

Paul sat in a Roman prison, his body weary from years of travel, persecution, and hardship. The cold stones pressed against him as he wrote to Timothy, his beloved companion in faith. Outside, the empire was strong and powerful, yet Paul's chains could not silence the message burning within him. He knew his life was nearing its end, but there was no fear in his words, only confidence in the God he had served faithfully.

He remembered the countless miles walked across dusty roads, carrying the gospel to cities and villages that had never heard the name of Jesus. He thought of the nights spent shipwrecked at sea, the times he was beaten and thrown into prison, the hours he worked with his own hands to provide for himself while preaching the Word. Through every trial, God's strength had sustained him.

Paul reflected on the moments of triumph as well. He recalled the joy of seeing churches grow, of watching hearts transformed by the Spirit, of baptizing new believers who once worshiped idols. These memories filled him with gratitude. His life had been poured out like a drink offering, given fully in service to Christ.

As he dipped his pen into the ink, he wrote words that would echo through generations: "I have fought the good fight, I have finished the race, I have kept the faith." For Paul, faith was not a sprint but a marathon, a lifelong commitment marked by endurance, courage, and perseverance. He knew his reward was not found in earthly treasures or recognition, but in the crown of righteousness that the Lord had prepared for him. The prison walls were closing in, but Paul's vision stretched far beyond. He saw eternity, the promise of being with Christ forever. His heart rested in the assurance that he had lived faithfully, and now he awaited the prize that no one could take away. Even in chains, Paul was free, because his life belonged to the One who had conquered death.

- Prayer: Lord, help me stay faithful to You through every season of life. Give me strength to keep running my race with perseverance.
- Reflecting Question: What does it mean for you to "fight the good fight" and "finish the race" in your own faith journey?
- Key Verse: "I have fought the good fight, I have finished the race, I have kept the faith." (2 Timothy 4:7)
- Faith in Action: Choose one spiritual goal and take a step toward it this week, no matter how small.
- Gratitude Prompt: Thank God for the faithful believers who have inspired you to keep going in your own race.

John's Vision of Heaven

John was on the island of Patmos when he received a vision unlike anything he had ever seen. Carried by the Spirit, he looked and saw a new heaven and a new earth. The old order of things had passed away. The sea, often a symbol of separation and fear, was gone.

Then John saw the Holy City, the new Jerusalem, coming down out of heaven from God. It was prepared like a bride beautifully dressed for her husband. The city shone with the glory of God, sparkling like a precious jewel. High walls surrounded it, with gates that were never closed, for there was no danger or night to fear.

A loud voice from the throne declared, "Look, God's dwelling place is now among the people, and He will dwell with them. They will be His people, and God Himself will be with them and be their God." John heard the promise that every tear would be wiped away. Death, mourning, crying, and pain would be no more. The former things had disappeared forever.

The One seated on the throne said, "I am making everything new." He told John to write these words down, for they were true and trustworthy. The water of life would flow freely to the thirsty, and those who overcame would inherit all these blessings. God Himself would be their Father, and they would be His children.

An angel carried John to a high mountain and showed him the city once more. It gleamed with streets of pure gold, clear as glass. The foundations of the city walls were decorated with every kind of precious stone. The gates were made of pearls, and light filled every corner, not from the sun or moon but from the glory of God and the Lamb.

In the city stood the river of the water of life, clear as crystal, flowing from the throne of God and of the Lamb. On each side of the river grew the tree of life, bearing fruit each month and leaves for the healing of the nations. No curse remained. God's servants saw His face, and His name was written on their foreheads. They reigned with Him forever and ever.

- Prayer: Lord, thank You for the hope of eternal life in Your presence.
- Reflecting Question: How does the promise of heaven give you comfort today?
- Key Verse: "He will wipe every tear from their eyes." (Revelation 21:4)
- Faith in Action: Encourage someone this week by reminding them of the hope of heaven.
- Gratitude Prompt: Write down three reasons you are thankful for eternal life.

Cain and Abel

Adam and Eve had two sons. Cain worked the soil, growing crops from the ground, while Abel took care of the flocks. When the time came to bring an offering to the Lord, Cain brought some of the fruits of the soil. Abel, however, chose the best portions from the firstborn of his flock. The Lord looked with favor on Abel and his offering, but Cain's offering did not please Him in the same way.

Cain's heart grew heavy with jealousy and anger. He saw the joy in Abel's eyes and the Lord's approval, and bitterness began to take root. God spoke to Cain and said, "Why are you angry? If you do what is right, will you not be accepted? But if you do not do what is right, sin is waiting at your door. It desires to have you, but you must rule over it."

Cain did not listen. He called his brother Abel out to the field. There, in a moment of rage and envy, Cain struck Abel down and killed him. The earth received Abel's blood, and Cain stood over the body of his brother, consumed by the weight of what he had done.

The Lord came to Cain and asked, "Where is your brother Abel?" Cain answered, "I don't know. Am I my brother's keeper?" But the Lord already knew. He said, "Your brother's blood cries out to me from the ground." God declared that Cain would be cursed. The ground would no longer yield its strength to him, and he would be a restless wanderer on the earth.

Cain cried out in despair. "My punishment is more than I can bear. Whoever finds me will kill me." But the Lord showed mercy even in judgment. He placed a mark on Cain so that no one who found him would harm him. Cain went out from the presence of the Lord and lived in the land of Nod, east of Eden. It was a story of envy, sin, and consequence, but also of God's justice mixed with mercy. Abel's life ended, yet his faithfulness still spoke. Cain's path turned dark, yet God did not abandon him completely.

- Prayer: Lord, help me guard my heart from jealousy and anger, and teach me to choose love instead.
- Reflecting Question: How do you usually respond when someone else succeeds or receives praise?
- Key Verse: "Sin is crouching at your door; it desires to have you, but you must rule over it." (Genesis 4:7)
- Faith in Action: Celebrate someone else's success this week instead of comparing yourself to them.
- Gratitude Prompt: Thank God for one unique gift He has given you.

The Tower of Babel

After the great flood, humanity grew again and spread across the land. At that time, the people all spoke one language and understood one another easily. As they moved eastward, they found a plain in the land of Shinar and decided to settle there.

With unity and ambition, they said to one another, "Come, let us make bricks and bake them thoroughly." They used brick instead of stone and tar instead of mortar. Their skills and cooperation gave them confidence, and soon their ideas grew larger.

Then the people said, "Come, let us build ourselves a city, with a tower that reaches to the heavens. Let us make a name for ourselves, so that we will not be scattered over the face of the whole earth."

Their goal was not simply to build but to elevate themselves. The tower would be a symbol of their greatness, a monument to human pride. Together they worked, brick upon brick, and the tower began to rise into the sky.

But the Lord looked down on the city and the tower the people were building. He saw their unity and their ambition. With one language and one purpose, nothing they planned would be impossible for them. Yet their hearts were not turned toward Him but toward their own glory.

The Lord said, "Come, let us go down and confuse their language so they will not understand each other." Suddenly, workers could not understand their neighbors. Commands turned into confusion. Bricklayers could not follow instructions. Arguments broke out, and progress came to a halt.

Unable to communicate, the people stopped building. The tower stood unfinished, a silent monument to their pride and the power of God to humble it. The Lord scattered them from there over all the earth, and the city was left behind.

That place became known as Babel, because there the Lord confused the language of the whole world. From there, humanity spread out in different directions, speaking many languages, carrying with them the reminder that their plans cannot replace God's purpose.

- Prayer: Lord, keep me humble and focused on glorifying You, not myself.
- Reflecting Question: When are you tempted to seek recognition instead of giving glory to God?
- Key Verse: "So the Lord scattered them from there over all the earth, and they stopped building the city." (Genesis 11:8)
- Faith in Action: Give credit to God or others this week instead of yourself.
- Gratitude Prompt: Thank God for the talents of others that inspire you.

Jacob and Esau

Jacob and Esau were twins, but they could not have been more different. Esau, the firstborn, grew up strong and skilled in hunting. Jacob was quieter, preferring to stay near the tents. Their father, Isaac, favored Esau, while their mother, Rebekah, loved Jacob more.

One day Esau came back from the fields exhausted and hungry. Jacob was cooking a pot of stew, and Esau begged for some. Jacob saw an opportunity and replied, "First sell me your birthright." Esau, too tired to think carefully, swore an oath and traded his birthright for a bowl of food. From that moment, Jacob held the right of the firstborn.

Years later, Isaac grew old and nearly blind. Knowing his time was short, he asked Esau to hunt game and prepare a meal so he could bless him. Rebekah overheard and quickly made a plan for Jacob to receive the blessing instead. She cooked food and dressed Jacob in Esau's clothes, even covering his hands with goat skins so he would feel like his hairy brother.

Jacob went to his father pretending to be Esau. Isaac hesitated but finally gave the blessing, believing it was his firstborn. Esau returned soon after, furious when he learned what had happened. His cry was filled with pain, and he vowed to kill Jacob.

Fearing for his life, Jacob fled to his uncle Laban's home. Years passed before the two brothers would see each other again. During that time Jacob married, had children, and grew wealthy, but he carried the memory of his deceit and the fear of Esau's anger.

Eventually, God called Jacob to return to his homeland. As he approached, Jacob heard that Esau was coming to meet him with four hundred men. Terrified, Jacob prayed and prepared gifts to soften his brother's heart. The night before their meeting, Jacob wrestled with a mysterious man until dawn and received a new name: Israel.

The next morning, Jacob saw Esau approaching. Instead of attacking, Esau ran to his brother, embraced him, and wept. The anger and bitterness were gone, replaced by forgiveness. The two brothers reconciled, showing that even deep wounds can be healed when God is at work.

- Prayer: Lord, help me seek peace and reconciliation in my relationships.
- Reflecting Question: Who in your life do you need to reconcile with?
- Key Verse: "Esau ran to meet Jacob and embraced him." (Genesis 33:4)
- Faith in Action: Take one small step toward peace with someone you've disagreed with.
- Gratitude Prompt: Thank God for a relationship that has been healed.

Joseph Forgives His Brothers

Years had passed since Joseph's brothers had sold him into slavery. They thought they had erased him from their lives, but God had raised Joseph to a position of great power in Egypt. When famine spread across the land, his brothers traveled to Egypt seeking food, never realizing that the governor who held their future in his hands was the brother they had once betrayed.

Joseph had tested them, watching how they treated their youngest brother, Benjamin. He saw their sorrow and their change of heart. When he could no longer hold back his emotions, Joseph ordered all the Egyptian attendants out of the room. Left alone with his brothers, his voice trembled as he revealed his identity.

"I am Joseph," he said. Shock swept across the room. Fear gripped his brothers, for they remembered the cruelty of their actions years before. Joseph, once the boy they had mocked and sold, now had the power to punish them.

But Joseph's eyes filled with tears, not anger. He stepped closer and spoke words of grace. "Do not be distressed and do not be angry with yourselves for selling me here, because it was to save lives that God sent me ahead of you." His brothers stood in silence, overwhelmed by the mercy they did not deserve.

Joseph embraced Benjamin first, then turned to each of his brothers. The years of separation melted away in those moments of forgiveness. The family that had been torn apart was restored.

Joseph explained how God had used their betrayal for a greater purpose. What they meant for harm, God had turned into a way to preserve many lives during the famine. Instead of bitterness, Joseph chose forgiveness. Instead of revenge, he offered reconciliation.

The brothers wept together, their voices echoing through the halls of the palace. For the first time in years, they stood united not by guilt or fear but by the grace of God. Joseph welcomed them into Egypt, providing food and safety for their families. The story that began with jealousy ended with forgiveness, showing that God's plan is always bigger than human failures.

- Prayer: Lord, give me the strength to forgive those who have hurt me deeply.
- Reflecting Question: Is there someone in your life you need to forgive even if it feels impossible?
- Key Verse: "You meant evil against me, but God meant it for good." (Genesis 50:20)
- Faith in Action: Write a short note of kindness or encouragement to someone you've struggled to forgive.
- Gratitude Prompt: Thank God for forgiving you completely through Jesus.

The Call of Gideon

The Israelites were living in fear. For seven years, the Midianites had raided their land, destroying crops and livestock. Every time the people planted their fields, the enemy came like swarms of locusts, leaving nothing behind. Many families hid in caves, afraid of being discovered. In the middle of this despair lived Gideon, a young man from the tribe of Manasseh.

One day Gideon was threshing wheat in a winepress, hiding from the Midianites so they would not steal his harvest. As he worked in secret, an angel of the Lord appeared and said, "The Lord is with you, mighty warrior." Gideon looked around in disbelief. He did not feel like a warrior. He saw himself as weak, from the smallest clan, and the least important in his family.

Gideon questioned the angel. "If the Lord is with us, why has all this happened to us? Where are the miracles our ancestors told us about?" The Lord answered him directly, "Go in the strength you have and save Israel out of Midian's hand. Am I not sending you?" Still, Gideon hesitated. He asked for a sign, and the angel touched his offering with the tip of his staff. Fire flared from the rock and consumed it. Gideon fell to the ground, realizing he had seen the messenger of God.

Even with the sign, Gideon still wrestled with doubt. Later, he laid out a fleece of wool, asking God to make it wet with dew while the ground stayed dry. God did it. The next night Gideon asked the opposite, and once again God answered. Patiently, God reassured him that he had indeed been chosen.

When the time came to fight, Gideon gathered thousands of men. But God told him the army was too large. He reduced it first by sending home those who were afraid, and then by separating the soldiers based on how they drank water from the river. In the end, Gideon was left with only three hundred men. That night, God gave Gideon courage. With trumpets, torches hidden in jars, and loud shouts, the three hundred surrounded the Midianite camp. Panic broke out among the enemy, and they turned their swords against each other. The great army that once terrified Israel was defeated, not by human strength, but by the power of God working through a hesitant young man.

- Prayer: Lord, help me trust Your strength when I feel weak.
- Reflecting Question: What insecurities hold you back from following God's call?
- Key Verse: "Go in the strength you have... Am I not sending you?" (Judges 6:14)
- Faith in Action: Take one small step this week in an area where you feel inadequate.
- Gratitude Prompt: Thank God for times He worked through your weakness.

Deborah the Judge

The people of Israel were living under oppression. For twenty years, the mighty army of King Jabin of Canaan and his commander, Sisera, had cruelly ruled over them. Fear had spread throughout the land, and the Israelites cried out to God for help. In this time of great need, God raised up Deborah as a judge over Israel.

Deborah was not only wise but also deeply faithful. She would sit under a palm tree between Ramah and Bethel, and people from all over came to her to settle disputes. She listened carefully, guided by God's Spirit, and gave judgments that brought peace and fairness.

One day, Deborah sent for Barak, a military leader from the tribe of Naphtali. She told him that God had commanded him to gather ten thousand men and lead them to Mount Tabor. God promised to deliver Sisera and his army into his hands. But Barak hesitated. He said he would only go if Deborah went with him. Deborah agreed but warned him that the honor of victory would not be his. Instead, God would deliver Sisera into the hands of a woman.

So Deborah went with Barak, and the men gathered for battle. When the time came, Deborah gave the order with boldness: "Go! This is the day the Lord has given Sisera into your hands." Encouraged by her words, Barak led his men down the slopes of Mount Tabor. At that very moment, God threw Sisera's army into confusion. The soldiers fled, and Barak's men struck them down.

Sisera, the commander, escaped on foot. Weary and desperate, he sought shelter in the tent of Jael, the wife of a Kenite. Jael welcomed him in, gave him milk, and covered him with a blanket. Believing he was safe, Sisera fell into a deep sleep. Then Jael took a tent peg and drove it through his temple, and Sisera died. In this way, the prophecy of Deborah was fulfilled: the victory went to a woman.

After the battle, Deborah and Barak sang a song of praise to the Lord. Their voices rose in thanksgiving for God's mighty hand that had freed Israel from oppression. Under Deborah's leadership, the land had peace for forty years.

- Prayer: Lord, give me wisdom and courage to lead when You call me.
- Reflecting Question: How can you be a leader for good in your school, family, or community?
- Key Verse: "Village life in Israel ceased, until I, Deborah, arose, a mother in Israel." (Judges 5:7)
- Faith in Action: Stand up for what is right in one situation this week, even if it feels difficult.
- Gratitude Prompt: Thank God for strong role models in your life who inspire you.

Hannah's Prayer

Hannah lived in a time when being unable to have children was seen as a heavy burden. She was married to Elkanah, a man who loved her deeply, but she carried the deep sorrow of not being able to conceive. To make matters worse, Elkanah's other wife mocked Hannah for her barrenness, leaving her heart wounded and her spirit broken.

Each year the family traveled to Shiloh to worship the Lord and offer sacrifices. On one of these trips, Hannah rose after the meal and went to the house of the Lord. Overwhelmed with grief, she poured out her heart in prayer. Her lips moved silently as she cried, asking God to give her a son. She made a vow that if God answered her prayer, she would dedicate the child to His service for all the days of his life.

The priest Eli noticed her praying and thought she was drunk because her lips moved without sound. Hannah explained that she was not drunk but pouring out her soul before the Lord. Touched by her sincerity, Eli told her to go in peace and may the Lord grant her request.

Hannah returned to her family, and her face was no longer downcast. She chose to trust that God had heard her. In time, the Lord remembered her, and she gave birth to a son. She named him Samuel, saying, "Because I asked the Lord for him."

True to her promise, when Samuel was old enough, Hannah brought him to Eli the priest. Though it must have been painful to leave her long-awaited child, she rejoiced in keeping her vow. She declared that Samuel would belong to the Lord for his whole life.

Hannah lifted a prayer of praise, glorifying God for His faithfulness. She celebrated not only the gift of a son but also the greatness of God who lifts up the humble. Her story became a testimony that God hears the cries of His people and answers in His perfect time.

- Prayer: Lord, teach me to pray with persistence and trust Your timing.
- Reflecting Question: When have you prayed for something for a long time, and how did it shape your faith?
- Key Verse: "For this child I prayed, and the Lord has granted me what I asked of him." (1 Samuel 1:27)
- Faith in Action: Commit to pray daily for one person or situation this week, trusting God with the outcome.
- Gratitude Prompt: Thank God for an answered prayer in your life.

Solomon's Wisdom

When Solomon became king after his father David, he was still a young man. The weight of ruling over Israel felt heavy on his shoulders. One night, Solomon had a dream in which the Lord appeared to him and said, "Ask for whatever you want me to give you."

Solomon could have asked for wealth, fame, or a long life. Instead, he humbled himself before God. He said, "Lord, You have made me king in place of my father David, but I am only a little child and do not know how to carry out my duties. Give Your servant a discerning heart to govern Your people and to distinguish between right and wrong."

God was pleased with Solomon's request. Because Solomon asked for wisdom rather than riches or power, God granted him not only great understanding but also honor and prosperity beyond what any other king would have.

Soon after, Solomon's wisdom was tested. Two women came before him, each claiming to be the mother of a baby boy. They both insisted that the child was theirs, and there were no witnesses to prove the truth. The people waited to see what Solomon would do.

Solomon called for a sword. "Cut the living child in two and give half to each woman," he said. The first woman agreed, but the second cried out, "Please, my lord, give her the living baby! Do not kill him!"

In that moment, Solomon knew who the true mother was. He ordered the baby to be given to the woman who was willing to give him up to save his life. News of Solomon's judgment spread quickly, and all Israel recognized that God had given their king extraordinary wisdom.

Under Solomon's leadership, Israel experienced peace and prosperity. His reputation grew beyond the borders of the nation. Kings and queens from distant lands came to hear his words and see the blessings God had given him. Solomon's wisdom became a sign of God's faithfulness to those who seek His guidance with humility.

- Prayer: Lord, give me wisdom to make good choices each day.
- Reflecting Question: What's one area where you need wisdom right now?
- Key Verse: "Give your servant a discerning heart to govern your people." (1 Kings 3:9)
- Faith in Action: Before making a decision this week, pause to pray for wisdom.
- Gratitude Prompt: Thank God for giving you guidance when you needed it.

Nehemiah Rebuilds the Wall

News reached Nehemiah, a Jewish man serving as cupbearer to King Artaxerxes in Persia, that the walls of Jerusalem lay in ruins and the gates had been burned. The people who lived there were vulnerable, surrounded by enemies and shame. Nehemiah's heart broke, and he wept, fasted, and prayed, asking God to forgive the sins of his people and to grant him favor before the king.

One day, while serving the king, Nehemiah's sadness could not be hidden. The king noticed and asked him why he was troubled. Nehemiah prayed quickly in his heart and then answered with courage. He told the king about the broken walls of his city. The king listened and granted Nehemiah permission to return to Jerusalem, even providing letters of protection and resources for the work.

When Nehemiah arrived, he inspected the ruins at night. He saw the collapsed stones and burned gates. Then he called the people together and said, "Come, let us rebuild the wall of Jerusalem, and we will no longer be in disgrace." The people agreed and set their hands to the work.

Not everyone was pleased. Enemies mocked them, saying they would fail. They threatened attacks and tried to frighten Nehemiah's workers. But Nehemiah stood firm. He encouraged the people to keep going and reminded them that God was with them. Half the men worked while the other half stood guard with swords and spears. Even those building the wall carried tools in one hand and weapons in the other.

Day after day, stone by stone, the wall began to rise again. Though the enemies plotted, their plans failed, because God's people stayed united and determined. After only fifty-two days, the wall was completed. The people celebrated, and even their enemies had to admit that this work had been done with the help of God.

Nehemiah's leadership and prayerful heart turned despair into hope. What once was broken now stood strong again, a sign of God's protection and faithfulness.

- Prayer: Lord, give me perseverance to keep building what You've called me to do.
- Reflecting Question: When have you faced obstacles while trying to finish something important?
- Key Verse: "The God of heaven will give us success. We his servants will start rebuilding." (Nehemiah 2:20)
- Faith in Action: Finish one task this week that you've been putting off, no matter how small.
- Gratitude Prompt: Thank God for giving you strength to complete something difficult in your life.

The Fiery Furnace

King Nebuchadnezzar built a golden statue that stood tall for all to see. He commanded that every person in the kingdom bow down and worship it whenever the sound of music filled the air. Anyone who refused would be thrown into a blazing furnace.

Among the people living in Babylon were three young men from Judah: Shadrach, Meshach, and Abednego. They had been taken from their homeland, but even in a foreign land they remained faithful to the God of Israel. When the music played and the crowd bowed before the statue, they stood tall. They would not bend their knees to an idol.

The king's officials noticed their defiance and quickly reported them. Furious, Nebuchadnezzar summoned the three men and gave them one more chance. "If you bow when you hear the music, all will be well," he warned. "But if you refuse, you will be thrown into the furnace. Then what god will be able to rescue you from my hand?"

Shadrach, Meshach, and Abednego answered with calm courage. "King Nebuchadnezzar, we do not need to defend ourselves before you in this matter. If we are thrown into the furnace, the God we serve is able to deliver us. But even if He does not, we will not serve your gods or worship the statue you have set up."

The king's face twisted with rage. He ordered the furnace heated seven times hotter than usual and commanded his strongest soldiers to tie the three men and throw them in. The fire was so fierce that the flames killed the soldiers who carried them, but Shadrach, Meshach, and Abednego fell bound into the furnace.

Nebuchadnezzar leapt to his feet in astonishment. "Didn't we throw three men into the fire? Look! I see four men walking around, unbound and unharmed, and the fourth looks like a son of the gods."

The king approached the furnace and called out, "Shadrach, Meshach, and Abednego, servants of the Most High God, come out!" They stepped out, their clothes unsinged, not even smelling of smoke. Nebuchadnezzar declared, "Praise be to the God of Shadrach, Meshach, and Abednego, who sent His angel and rescued His servants. No other god can save in this way."

- Prayer: Lord, give me courage to stand firm in my faith even when I feel pressured to compromise.
- Reflecting Question: What pressures in your life tempt you to compromise your faith?
- Key Verse: "The God we serve is able to deliver us from it, and he will deliver us from Your Majesty's hand." (Daniel 3:17)
- Faith in Action: Say no to one negative influence this week, even if it feels difficult.
- Gratitude Prompt: Thank God for one time He stood with you during a hard moment.

Daniel Interprets the King's Dream

King Nebuchadnezzar of Babylon was troubled by a strange dream that none of his advisors could explain. In his frustration, he demanded not only the interpretation but also that the wise men tell him what he had dreamed. If they failed, they would be put to death. The demand was impossible, and fear spread among the wise men of Babylon.

Among them was Daniel, a young man from Judah who served in the king's court. When he heard the decree, he asked for time to seek an answer. That night, Daniel gathered his friends Hananiah, Mishael, and Azariah, and together they prayed earnestly to God for mercy and wisdom.

During the night, God revealed the king's dream to Daniel in a vision. The next morning, Daniel praised the Lord, declaring that wisdom and power belong to Him, and that He reveals deep and hidden things. Strengthened by God's answer, Daniel went before the king.

Daniel told Nebuchadnezzar what he had dreamed. He described a massive statue with a head of gold, chest and arms of silver, belly and thighs of bronze, legs of iron, and feet made of iron mixed with clay. Then, a stone cut without human hands struck the statue, shattering it completely. The stone grew into a great mountain that filled the earth.

Daniel explained the meaning: the head of gold represented the king and his kingdom. After him would come other kingdoms, each inferior to the one before, until a divided kingdom of iron and clay. Finally, God would establish His own kingdom, eternal and unshakable, that no human power could destroy.

As Nebuchadnezzar listened, his face changed from suspicion to awe. He knew that only the true God could reveal such a mystery. Falling before Daniel, the king honored him and acknowledged that Daniel's God was the God of gods and the Lord of kings. He elevated Daniel to a high position in Babylon and granted him authority over many affairs.

What began as a death sentence became a moment of glory for God. Daniel's faith and courage showed that even in a foreign land, far from home, the God of heaven rules over all kings and kingdoms.

- Prayer: Lord, give me understanding and wisdom when I face confusion.
- Reflecting Question: When have you needed God's help to understand a situation?
- Key Verse: "He reveals deep and hidden things." (Daniel 2:22)
- Faith in Action: Pray for God's guidance before making one decision this week.
- Gratitude Prompt: Thank God for giving you clarity in a confusing moment.

Daniel's Integrity

When the people of Judah were taken captive to Babylon, many young men were chosen to serve in the king's palace. Among them was Daniel, along with his friends Hananiah, Mishael, and Azariah. They were intelligent and strong, and the king's officials prepared them to be trained for royal service. Part of their preparation included eating the food from the king's table and drinking his wine. At first glance, this might have seemed like an honor. The king's food was rich and luxurious, but it was also against the laws God had given the Israelites. Some of it may have been offered to idols, and some was not prepared according to God's instructions. For Daniel, eating it would mean compromising his faith.

Daniel made a quiet but firm decision. He resolved in his heart not to defile himself with the royal food and wine. Instead, he asked the chief official for permission to eat only vegetables and drink water. The official was hesitant. He worried that if Daniel and his friends looked weak, the king would punish him. Daniel responded with wisdom and humility. He suggested a test: for ten days, he and his friends would eat only vegetables and drink water, while the others continued with the royal food. After that time, the official could compare their health and decide what was best.

The official agreed, and the test began. For ten days, Daniel and his friends ate simple food and drank only water. At the end of the trial, they looked healthier and stronger than all the other young men who had eaten the king's rich meals. Seeing this, the official allowed them to continue their diet.

God honored Daniel's integrity and gave him and his friends knowledge and understanding beyond all the others in the king's service. Daniel's resolve to remain faithful in small things prepared him for greater challenges later in his life. He proved that even in a foreign land, surrounded by pressure to conform, he could stay true to God.

Daniel's story is a reminder that faithfulness often begins with small choices. His courage to stand firm without compromise made him a shining example for generations to come.

- Prayer: Lord, help me stay true to my values even under pressure.
- Reflecting Question: What temptations make it hard for you to stay true to your faith?
- Key Verse: "But Daniel resolved not to defile himself with the royal food and wine." (Daniel 1:8)
- Faith in Action: Make one choice this week that honors God, even if it's unpopular.
- Gratitude Prompt: Thank God for helping you stand firm in a past challenge.

Jonah's Mission to Nineveh

Jonah had already experienced God's mercy in a way few could imagine. After running away from the command to preach in Nineveh, he had been thrown into the sea and swallowed by a great fish. Inside the darkness of its belly, he prayed with all his heart, and God gave him a second chance. When the fish released him on the shore, Jonah knew he could not ignore the Lord again.

The word of the Lord came to Jonah a second time. "Go to the great city of Nineveh and proclaim to it the message I give you." Jonah obeyed and set out for the city. Nineveh was vast, taking three days to cross, its streets crowded with merchants, families, soldiers, and idols. Jonah walked into the heart of the city and began to proclaim, "Forty more days and Nineveh will be overthrown."

His words carried through the busy markets and into the homes of the people. At first, some mocked him, but as the message spread, a wave of fear and conviction fell on the city. People began to whisper to one another that this man's God was powerful and that destruction could be near.

The news reached the king of Nineveh. He rose from his throne, removed his royal robe, and covered himself in sackcloth. He sat in ashes, a sign of humility and grief. Then he issued a decree throughout the city: "Do not let people or animals, herds or flocks, taste anything. Do not let them eat or drink. Let everyone call urgently on God. Let them give up their evil ways and their violence. Who knows? God may yet relent and with compassion turn from his fierce anger so that we will not perish."

From the poorest laborer to the nobles in the palace, all of Nineveh turned to fasting and repentance. Streets once filled with noise grew quiet as families prayed together, pleading for mercy.

When God saw what they did and how they turned from their evil ways, He had compassion. He did not bring the destruction He had threatened. Instead, He spared the city, showing that His mercy is greater than judgment when hearts truly change.

Jonah's reluctant obedience had led to the salvation of an entire city. Nineveh, known for its violence and pride, now bowed before the Lord, living proof of what can happen when God's message is heard and hearts are willing to turn back to Him.

- Prayer: Lord, help me obey quickly and share Your message of love.
- Reflecting Question: When have you experienced a second chance from God?
- Key Verse: "When God saw what they did and how they turned from their evil ways, he relented." (Jonah 3:10)
- Faith in Action: Share an encouraging message with someone who needs hope.
- Gratitude Prompt: Thank God for His patience with you.

The Faith of Job

Job lived in the land of Uz, a man known for his righteousness and devotion to God. He was blessed with wealth, flocks, servants, and a large family. He regularly offered sacrifices for his children, wanting to keep them close to God. Job's life seemed secure, full of peace and blessing.

One day, however, a great test began. In a single series of tragedies, Job lost his oxen, donkeys, and servants to raiders. Soon after, fire from the sky consumed his sheep. Not long after, another messenger came with news that his camels had been stolen. Worst of all, a final servant arrived trembling with the report that a violent wind had struck the house where Job's sons and daughters were feasting, and the building collapsed. All of his children were gone in an instant.

Overwhelmed by grief, Job tore his robe, shaved his head, and fell to the ground in worship. Through tears he said, "The Lord gave and the Lord has taken away; may the name of the Lord be praised." Even in the face of unthinkable loss, he did not sin by blaming God.

But Job's trial was not over. His health soon failed. Painful sores broke out across his body from the soles of his feet to the crown of his head. He sat among ashes, scraping his skin with a shard of pottery. His wife, seeing his suffering, urged him to curse God and give up. But Job replied, "Shall we accept good from God, and not trouble?" Still, he did not turn away from his faith.

Three of Job's friends came to comfort him. At first they sat in silence, weeping with him. But then they began to argue, suggesting that Job's suffering must have been punishment for hidden sins. Job defended his innocence, insisting that he had lived faithfully. Yet the questions in his heart grew heavier. He longed for answers from God, but none seemed to come.

Finally, God spoke out of a storm. He reminded Job of His power in creation, His wisdom, and His sovereignty over all things. Job realized that he had spoken of things too wonderful for him to understand. Humbled, he confessed his trust in God once again.

In the end, God restored Job's fortunes. He blessed him with twice as much as before, gave him new sons and daughters, and granted him a long life. Job's story became a testimony of endurance, showing that faith can survive even the deepest trials.

- Prayer: Lord, help me trust You even when life feels unfair and painful.
- Reflecting Question: How do you usually respond when everything seems to go wrong?
- Key Verse: "Though he slay me, yet will I hope in him." (Job 13:15)
- Faith in Action: Encourage someone this week who is facing difficulties.
- Gratitude Prompt: Thank God for one blessing you still have, even in hard times.

The Faith of Abraham

Abraham had waited many years for the son God had promised. When Isaac was finally born, he brought joy and laughter into Abraham's home. Isaac grew into a boy full of life, and Abraham loved him deeply. He was the child of promise, the one through whom God's covenant would continue.

One day, God spoke to Abraham in a way that must have shaken his heart. "Take your son, your only son Isaac, whom you love, and go to the region of Moriah. Sacrifice him there as a burnt offering on a mountain I will show you."

The command seemed impossible. Isaac was the miracle child, the answer to years of prayer. Yet Abraham rose early the next morning, saddled his donkey, and took Isaac and two servants with him. For three days they traveled until they saw the mountain in the distance. Abraham told the servants to stay behind while he and Isaac went on alone.

Isaac carried the wood for the sacrifice on his back, while Abraham carried the fire and the knife. As they walked together, Isaac asked, "Father, the fire and wood are here, but where is the lamb for the burnt offering?"

Abraham answered with faith that must have trembled on his lips: "God himself will provide the lamb, my son."

When they reached the place God had shown him, Abraham built an altar and arranged the wood. He tied his son Isaac and laid him on the altar. With tears and courage mingled, he reached out his hand and took the knife to slay his son.

At that moment, the angel of the Lord called out from heaven, "Abraham! Abraham!" He replied, "Here I am." The angel said, "Do not lay a hand on the boy. Now I know that you fear God, because you have not withheld from me your son, your only son."

Abraham looked up and saw a ram caught by its horns in a thicket. He took the ram and sacrificed it instead of his son. He named that place "The Lord Will Provide." God confirmed His promise, saying Abraham's descendants would be as countless as the stars in the sky and the sand on the seashore. Because Abraham trusted and obeyed, blessings would flow through his family to the entire world.

- Prayer: Lord, help me trust You completely, even when I don't understand.
- Reflecting Question: What's one area of your life that's hard to surrender to God?
- Key Verse: "The Lord will provide." (Genesis 22:14)
- Faith in Action: Surrender one worry to God in prayer this week.
- Gratitude Prompt: Thank God for providing for you in a surprising way.

Isaac and Rebekah

Abraham had grown old, and he wanted his son Isaac to have a wife from among his own people, not from the Canaanites around him. He called his most trusted servant and gave him a serious mission. "Go to my country and to my relatives. Find a wife for my son Isaac." The servant swore an oath to carry out his master's wish and set out on the long journey, taking camels and gifts with him.

After many days of travel, the servant reached a town near Nahor. Tired and hopeful, he stopped by a well outside the city as evening approached, when women came to draw water. There he prayed quietly, asking God for a clear sign. "Lord, God of my master Abraham, make me successful today. May the young woman I ask for a drink not only give me water but also offer to water my camels. Let that be the one You have chosen for Isaac."

Before he had finished praying, a young woman named Rebekah came to the well with her jar on her shoulder. She was very beautiful and, more importantly, kind. The servant ran to meet her. "Please, may I have a little water from your jar?" Rebekah quickly lowered her jar and gave him a drink. Then, without being asked, she said, "I will draw water for your camels too, until they have had enough."

She hurried back and forth, filling the trough until the thirsty animals were satisfied. The servant watched in amazement, knowing God had answered his prayer. He gave her gifts of gold jewelry and asked whose daughter she was. When Rebekah told him she was the granddaughter of Nahor, Abraham's brother, the servant bowed and praised God for guiding him directly to Abraham's family.

That evening he was welcomed into Rebekah's household, where he explained his mission and how God had led him. Her family recognized God's hand in the matter and agreed that Rebekah should go with him. The next morning, though it meant leaving her home behind, Rebekah willingly said, "I will go."

So Rebekah traveled with the servant back to Canaan. As they approached, Isaac was walking in the fields. When he saw her, he welcomed her, and she became his wife. Together they began a new chapter of God's promise to Abraham, a story of faith and divine guidance.

- Prayer: Lord, guide me in my relationships and future choices, and help me trust that You know what is best for me.
- Reflecting Question: How can you trust God with your future plans?
- Key Verse: "The Lord has led me on the journey to the house of my master's relatives." (Genesis 24:27)
- Faith in Action: Pray specifically about one decision you're facing this week and trust God to lead you.
- Gratitude Prompt: Thank God for guiding you in a past decision.

The Birth of Samuel

Hannah lived with a deep sadness. Year after year, she longed for a child, yet her arms remained empty. Though her husband tried to comfort her, nothing could take away the ache she carried in her heart. Still, Hannah did not give up hope. She brought her pain before God in prayer, pouring out her soul at the temple.

One day, as she wept silently, her lips moved but no sound came out. Eli, the priest, saw her and thought she was drunk. But when she explained her sorrow, Eli understood and blessed her, telling her that God had heard her request. Hannah left the temple with peace in her heart, even though her circumstances had not yet changed.

In time, God answered her prayer. Hannah gave birth to a son and named him Samuel, saying, "Because I asked the Lord for him." Her heart overflowed with joy. She knew that Samuel was not only her child but a gift from God.

Before Samuel was even born, Hannah had made a promise. If God gave her a son, she would dedicate him to the Lord's service for his whole life. When the time came, she did not turn back from her vow. After Samuel was weaned, she brought him to the temple and presented him to Eli. With reverence and gratitude, she declared, "I prayed for this child, and the Lord has granted me what I asked of him. So now I give him to the Lord."

Hannah's act of surrender was not easy. She loved Samuel deeply, yet she trusted that God's plan for him was greater than her own. Each year she would visit Samuel, bringing him a little robe she had made with her own hands. As Samuel grew, he served faithfully in the temple, and the Lord's favor was with him.

Hannah's story became one of answered prayer and fulfilled promises. Her tears had turned into joy, and her faith had left a legacy that would impact all of Israel. Samuel would one day become a prophet who guided kings and spoke God's word to the nation. And it all began with the prayer of a woman who refused to give up on God.

- Prayer: Lord, help me trust that You hear my prayers and answer them in Your perfect time.
- Reflecting Question: What prayer request have you been waiting patiently for God to answer?
- Key Verse: "For this child I prayed, and the Lord has granted me what I asked of him." (1 Samuel 1:27)
- Faith in Action: Write down one prayer request and keep bringing it to God each day this week.
- Gratitude Prompt: Thank God for a specific prayer He has already answered in your life.

Elisha and the Widow's Oil

The widow stood at the doorway of her small home, her eyes heavy with worry. Her husband, a man who had served faithfully among the prophets, had died. Now the creditors were demanding payment. With nothing left to offer, she feared her two sons would be taken as slaves. Desperation pushed her to seek out the prophet Elisha.

When she poured out her heart to him, Elisha listened carefully. He asked her a simple question: "What do you have in your house?" The widow lowered her eyes. "Nothing at all," she whispered, then added, "except a small jar of olive oil."

Elisha nodded and gave her instructions that must have sounded unusual. "Go to all your neighbors. Ask them for empty jars, as many as you can. Then go inside your house with your sons, shut the door, and pour oil into all the jars. Set each one aside as it is filled."

The widow hurried home and told her sons what the prophet had said. They scattered through the village, knocking on doors, asking for jars of every size and shape. Soon the floor of their little home was covered with containers. With trembling hands, the widow picked up her small jar and began to pour.

To her astonishment, the oil flowed steadily, filling the first jar. She set it aside and picked up another. Again, the oil poured out, smooth and rich, until that jar too was full. Her sons watched in amazement, handing her one jar after another. Each time, the oil kept flowing. Their excitement grew as jar after jar brimmed with oil, yet the little vessel in her hand never ran dry.

At last, she called out, "Bring me another jar!" Her sons looked around the room and shook their heads. "There are no more left." At that very moment, the oil stopped flowing.

Breathless, the widow went back to Elisha and told him everything that had happened. He smiled and said, "Go, sell the oil and pay your debts. You and your sons can live on what is left."

Her home, once filled with fear and emptiness, was now overflowing with provision. God had taken the little she had and turned it into more than enough.

- Prayer: Lord, thank You for providing for me even when I feel empty and overwhelmed. Help me to trust that You are always enough.
- Reflecting Question: What need in your life do you want to bring before God today?
- Key Verse: "The oil stopped flowing." (2 Kings 4:6)
- Faith in Action: Share something small you have with someone in need this week.
- Gratitude Prompt: Thank God for His provision in your family.

Elisha Heals Naaman

Naaman was a powerful commander in the army of Aram. He was respected by his king and feared by enemies, for victory often followed wherever he led his soldiers. Yet beneath his polished armor and commanding presence, Naaman carried a secret that weighed heavily on him. He suffered from leprosy, a disease that brought pain, shame, and isolation. No matter how great his victories, this sickness was a battle he could not win.

Among his household servants was a young girl from Israel, taken captive during a raid. Despite her circumstances, she spoke with kindness. One day she told Naaman's wife, "If only my master would see the prophet in Samaria. He would cure him of his leprosy." These words sparked a hope Naaman had not felt in years. With permission from his king, he gathered gifts and letters of introduction and set out for Israel.

Naaman arrived with his entourage at the house of Elisha, the prophet. Instead of coming out to greet him, Elisha sent a messenger with simple instructions: "Go, wash yourself seven times in the Jordan River, and your flesh will be restored." Naaman was furious. He had expected dramatic prayers, perhaps a hand raised to the heavens, something fitting for a man of his rank. The Jordan River seemed ordinary, even dirty compared to the rivers of his own land. In his pride, Naaman turned away in anger, ready to abandon the chance for healing.

But his servants approached him gently. "My father," they said, "if the prophet had told you to do something great, would you not have done it? How much more then, when he tells you simply to wash and be cleansed?" Their words humbled Naaman. Swallowing his pride, he went down to the Jordan. Once, twice, three times he dipped beneath the water. Each time he rose, the disease still clung to him. Four, five, six times—nothing had changed. But on the seventh time, as he came up from the water, his skin was clean, smooth like that of a child. The leprosy was gone. Overwhelmed with awe and gratitude, Naaman returned to Elisha. Standing before the prophet, he declared, "Now I know that there is no God in all the world except in Israel." Naaman's healing was more than physical. In that moment, he experienced the power of humility, obedience, and the mercy of the living God.

- Prayer: Lord, help me obey You even when I do not fully understand.
- Reflecting Question: What small step of obedience might God be asking you to take?
- Key Verse: "His flesh was restored and became clean like that of a young boy." (2 Kings 5:14)
- Faith in Action: Choose one simple instruction from God's Word and put it into practice this week.
- Gratitude Prompt: Thank God for one time He brought healing or renewal into your life.

The Call of Jeremiah

Jeremiah was still a young man when he first heard the voice of the Lord speaking directly to him. Life in his hometown of Anathoth was simple, and he never expected to be chosen for anything extraordinary. Yet one day God's words came with clarity and weight: "Before I formed you in the womb, I knew you. Before you were born, I set you apart. I appointed you as a prophet to the nations."

The message startled Jeremiah. He felt too inexperienced, too ordinary, too young for such a calling. Fear filled his heart, and his immediate response was an objection. "Alas, Sovereign Lord, I do not know how to speak; I am too young." His mind raced with doubts. How could he stand before leaders, priests, and kings? Who would listen to someone like him?

But God was not limited by Jeremiah's weakness or age. With steady authority, the Lord replied, "Do not say, 'I am too young.' You must go to everyone I send you to and say whatever I command you. Do not be afraid of them, for I am with you and will rescue you." These words carried both command and comfort. God was not only appointing Jeremiah but also promising His constant presence.

Then the Lord reached out His hand and touched Jeremiah's mouth. In that holy moment, Jeremiah felt the weight of his calling but also the strength of divine assurance. God declared, "I have put my words in your mouth. See, today I appoint you over nations and kingdoms to uproot and tear down, to destroy and overthrow, to build and to plant."

The task was heavy, yet the touch of God gave Jeremiah courage. His story would not be one of ease, but of faithfulness. He would face rejection, opposition, and loneliness, but he would never be abandoned. The God who had known him before birth was the same God who would sustain him every step of the way.

Jeremiah's calling reminds us that God chooses not based on age, skill, or status, but on His own purpose. What seemed impossible for Jeremiah became possible because God Himself was with him. From that day forward, Jeremiah stepped into the role of prophet, carrying the Word of the Lord to people and nations, proving that God's call is stronger than any fear.

- Prayer: Lord, give me courage to follow Your call, even when I feel too young or unprepared.
- Reflecting Question: What excuses do you make when God asks you to do something difficult?
- Key Verse: "Do not say, 'I am too young.' You must go to everyone I send you and say whatever I command you." (Jeremiah 1:7)
- Faith in Action: Take on one responsibility this week with courage, trusting that God is with you.
- Gratitude Prompt: Thank God for giving you a purpose, no matter your age or experience.

The Call of Moses

Moses had fled from Egypt years earlier and was living quietly as a shepherd in the land of Midian. Day after day he led his father-in-law's sheep through the wilderness, far from the royal courts where he had once grown up. One day, while guiding the flock near Mount Horeb, Moses noticed something strange. A bush was on fire, yet it was not burning up.

Curious, he stepped closer to see why the flames did not consume the branches. Suddenly, a voice called to him from the fire, "Moses, Moses." Afraid, Moses answered, "Here I am."

"Do not come any closer," the voice said. "Take off your sandals, for the place where you are standing is holy ground." Moses trembled as he realized he was in the presence of the Lord God. Covering his face, he listened as God declared, "I have seen the misery of my people in Egypt. I have heard their cries and I know their suffering. I have come down to rescue them and bring them into a good land."

Moses stood in silence, overwhelmed by what he was hearing. Then God spoke again, "So now, go. I am sending you to Pharaoh to bring my people, the Israelites, out of Egypt."

Moses' heart pounded. "Who am I, that I should go to Pharaoh and bring the Israelites out of Egypt?" he asked. He remembered his failures, his fears, and his past mistakes. But God answered with assurance, "I will be with you."

Still, Moses struggled. "Suppose I go to the Israelites and say, 'The God of your fathers has sent me,' and they ask me, 'What is his name?' What shall I tell them?"

God replied, "I AM WHO I AM. Tell them, 'I AM has sent me to you.'"

Even after hearing these words, Moses hesitated. He worried the people would not believe him. God showed him signs: his staff turning into a snake, his hand becoming leprous and then healed. Yet Moses still resisted. "Pardon your servant, Lord. I have never been eloquent. I am slow of speech and tongue." The Lord said, "Who gave human beings their mouths? Who makes them deaf or mute? Who gives them sight or makes them blind? Is it not I, the Lord? Now go; I will help you speak and will teach you what to say." Finally, God appointed Aaron, Moses' brother, to be his spokesman. With God's promise and Aaron's help, Moses accepted the call to return to Egypt and lead God's people out of slavery.

- Prayer: Lord, help me trust that You can use me despite my weaknesses.
- Reflecting Question: What excuses do you make when God calls you to act?
- Key Verse: "I will be with you." (Exodus 3:12)
- Faith in Action: Step into one responsibility this week even if you feel unprepared.
- Gratitude Prompt: Thank God for giving you courage in your weakness.

The Bronze Serpent

The Israelites continued their long journey through the wilderness, walking under the hot desert sun. Day after day, they grew weary of the sand, the hunger, and the endless waiting. Instead of trusting God, they began to complain. They spoke harshly against Moses and against the Lord, saying that they were tired of the manna and tired of the path set before them.

Their words showed hearts full of impatience and bitterness. Rather than gratitude, they chose grumbling. In response, God allowed poisonous snakes to come among the people. The snakes bit many, and those who were bitten grew weak and began to die. Fear spread through the camp as the people realized how serious their rebellion had been.

The Israelites rushed to Moses in desperation. "We have sinned," they admitted. "We spoke against the Lord and against you. Pray that He will take the snakes away from us." For the first time, they confessed their guilt and asked for mercy. Moses, faithful once again, prayed to God on their behalf.

The Lord gave Moses a strange instruction. He told him to make a serpent out of bronze and lift it high on a pole for everyone to see. Whoever had been bitten by a snake could look at the bronze serpent and live. It was not the bronze figure that had power, but God's promise attached to it. He provided a way for healing in the very midst of judgment.

Moses obeyed. He shaped a serpent out of bronze and placed it on a tall pole where it could be seen from every corner of the camp. When someone was bitten, they lifted their eyes toward the bronze serpent, trusting the word that God had given. And each one who looked lived. Strength returned to their bodies, and fear was replaced with relief.

This moment marked another turning point for Israel. It showed them that even when their hearts wandered, God's mercy was still greater than their failures. The people who had once complained now saw that life could only be found by trusting the Lord. The wilderness was still difficult, but they were reminded that God's way always leads to life.

- Prayer: Lord, help me look to You for healing and hope when I feel weak or afraid.
- Reflecting Question: Where do you usually turn first when you are hurting or in trouble?
- Key Verse: "So Moses made a bronze snake and put it up on a pole. Then when anyone was bitten by a snake and looked at the bronze snake, they lived." (Numbers 21:9)
- Faith in Action: This week, instead of trying to fix a struggle on your own, pause and ask God for help.
- Gratitude Prompt: Thank God for one time He brought healing or restoration into your life.

The Walls of Jericho

The Israelites had finally crossed the Jordan River and entered the land God had promised them. Their first challenge stood tall and intimidating before them: the fortified city of Jericho. Its massive walls seemed impossible to overcome. Soldiers guarded the gates, and no one could enter or leave. The people of Israel looked at the towering walls and wondered how victory could ever be possible. Joshua, their leader, sought the Lord for guidance. One night, he encountered a mysterious man standing with a drawn sword. Joshua asked, "Are you for us or for our enemies?" The man replied, "Neither, but as commander of the army of the Lord I have now come." Joshua fell facedown in reverence. The commander told him that the Lord had already given Jericho into his hands, but the battle would not be fought in the usual way.

God gave Joshua unusual instructions. For six days, the army was to march once around the city with the priests carrying the Ark of the Covenant. Seven priests were to carry trumpets made of rams' horns. No one was to shout, no one was to raise their voice. The people were simply to march in silence while the trumpets sounded.

On the seventh day, they were to march around the city seven times. After the seventh circle, the priests would give one long blast on the trumpets. Then all the people were to shout as loud as they could, and the walls of Jericho would collapse. Joshua relayed these instructions to the people, and though they must have seemed strange, they obeyed.

Day after day, the Israelites marched around the city in silence. The people of Jericho watched from the walls, mocking and jeering, but Israel did not respond. On the seventh day, the priests blew their trumpets as they circled the city again and again. With each lap the anticipation grew. At the seventh time, the priests gave one long blast, and Joshua commanded, "Shout! For the Lord has given you the city!" The people lifted their voices with a great shout. Suddenly the ground shook, and the mighty walls of Jericho crumbled to the ground. The soldiers rushed in, and the city was captured exactly as the Lord had promised. What had seemed impossible was made possible by faith and obedience to God's command.

- Prayer: Lord, teach me to trust Your ways even when they seem unusual.
- Reflecting Question: When have you struggled to trust God's plan because it didn't make sense?
- Key Verse: "By faith the walls of Jericho fell." (Hebrews 11:30)
- Faith in Action: Obey God in one small thing this week, even if it feels strange.
- Gratitude Prompt: Thank God for one time obedience brought blessing.

The Song of Mary

Mary was a young woman living in the small town of Nazareth when her life was suddenly transformed. The angel Gabriel had visited her with astonishing news: she would bear a child, conceived by the Holy Spirit, and this child would be the Son of God. Though surprised and humbled, Mary accepted God's plan with faith, saying, "I am the Lord's servant. May your word to me be fulfilled." Soon after, Mary traveled to visit her relative Elizabeth, who was also expecting a miraculous child in her old age. The moment Mary entered Elizabeth's home and greeted her, Elizabeth's baby leapt in the womb. Filled with the Holy Spirit, Elizabeth exclaimed, "Blessed are you among women, and blessed is the child you will bear!" She recognized that Mary carried the Savior promised by God.

Hearing Elizabeth's words, Mary's heart overflowed with gratitude and awe. She lifted her voice in a song of praise that has echoed through generations. "My soul glorifies the Lord, and my spirit rejoices in God my Savior," she began. Mary rejoiced that God had looked upon her, a humble servant, and chosen her to play a role in His great plan. She marveled at His power and mercy, declaring that all generations would call her blessed, not because of her own greatness, but because of what God had done.

Mary's song rose with powerful words about God's character. She proclaimed that He had scattered the proud, brought down rulers from their thrones, and lifted up the humble. He had filled the hungry with good things and sent the rich away empty. She rejoiced that God's promises to Israel, spoken long ago to Abraham and his descendants, were being fulfilled through the child she carried.

Mary's voice was steady and strong as she praised the faithfulness of God. Her song was not only personal but also a declaration of hope for her people. It was the anthem of someone who believed that God's mercy stretches from generation to generation. In that moment, she embodied both humility and courage, offering herself as a vessel for God's work.

The young woman from Nazareth, who had once lived quietly in the shadows of a small village, now stood at the center of the greatest story in history. Her song of praise was both intimate and universal, a reminder that God sees the lowly, keeps His promises, and turns the world upside down with His love.

- Prayer: Lord, fill my heart with gratitude and worship like Mary's.
- Reflecting Question: How can you practice gratitude even in uncertain times?
- Key Verse: "My soul glorifies the Lord and my spirit rejoices in God my Savior." (Luke 1:46–47)
- Faith in Action: Write your own short prayer of praise this week.
- Gratitude Prompt: Thank God for one blessing that surprised you.

The Shepherds Visit Jesus

That night in the fields near Bethlehem, a group of shepherds kept watch over their flocks. The air was cool and quiet, broken only by the sounds of sheep moving softly in the grass. These men were ordinary, not famous or powerful, yet it was to them that God chose to reveal something extraordinary.

Suddenly the stillness of the night was shattered. A brilliant light filled the sky, and an angel of the Lord appeared before them. The shepherds trembled, shielding their faces in fear. But the angel spoke gently, "Do not be afraid. I bring you good news that will cause great joy for all the people. Today in the town of David a Savior has been born to you; he is the Messiah, the Lord."

The angel told them how they would find the child—wrapped in cloths and lying in a manger. As soon as the message was given, the heavens burst open with the voices of a great company of angels praising God: "Glory to God in the highest heaven, and on earth peace to those on whom his favor rests."

The shepherds stood in awe as the sky glowed with the praise of heaven. Then, as suddenly as it appeared, the light faded, and the night grew still again. The shepherds looked at one another, their hearts racing. Without hesitation they said, "Let's go to Bethlehem and see this thing that has happened, which the Lord has told us about."

They hurried through the quiet streets until they found the stable. Just as the angel had said, there was a newborn baby lying in a manger, wrapped in simple cloth. His mother Mary and Joseph sat beside Him, watching over the child with gentle care.

The shepherds knelt down, overwhelmed by the wonder of the moment. They told Mary and Joseph everything the angels had said. Mary listened carefully, treasuring each word in her heart.

Afterward, the shepherds left the stable filled with joy. As they returned to their fields, they could not keep silent. They praised God and told everyone they met about the amazing things they had seen and heard. All who listened were astonished by their story. The shepherds went back to their ordinary lives, but they were never the same again. The night that had begun in darkness had been filled with heaven's light, and they carried that joy with them wherever they went.

- Prayer: Lord, help me share the joy of Your good news with others.
- Reflecting Question: Who can you share the message of Jesus with this week?
- Key Verse: "I bring you good news that will cause great joy for all the people." (Luke 2:10)
- Faith in Action: Share something joyful about your faith with a friend.
- Gratitude Prompt: Thank God for bringing joy into your life.

The Magi Visit Jesus

Far to the east, wise men studied the stars. They were scholars and seekers, men who watched the skies for signs. One night, they noticed something unlike anything they had ever seen before: a brilliant new star shining brightly against the dark sky. They believed it signaled the birth of a great king. With determination, they began a long journey, carrying precious gifts to honor the one they hoped to find.

Their path was not simple. Days turned into weeks as they crossed deserts and mountains. The sun burned during the day, and the cold pierced at night, but still they pressed on. Their goal was clear. They wanted to see the newborn King.

At last, the magi arrived in Jerusalem. They began to ask, "Where is the one who has been born King of the Jews? We saw his star when it rose and have come to worship him." Their question disturbed King Herod, who feared losing his throne. He gathered the priests and teachers of the law to find out where the Messiah was to be born. The answer was Bethlehem, a small village prophesied long ago.

Herod called the magi to him secretly. He told them, "Go and search carefully for the child. As soon as you find him, report to me, so that I too may go and worship him." But in his heart, Herod had no desire to worship. He planned to destroy this new King.

The magi left Jerusalem, and to their joy, the star they had seen earlier appeared again. It guided them directly to the house where Mary and Joseph were staying with the young child. Their long journey was finally complete. They entered the home, and when they saw Jesus with his mother Mary, they bowed down and worshiped him. This child, small and humble, was the King they had sought.

From their treasures, they presented gifts fit for royalty: gold, frankincense, and myrrh. Each gift held meaning, though they may not have fully understood it. Gold for a king, frankincense for worship, and myrrh for sacrifice. Their offering was not just of wealth, but of reverence.

That night, God warned the magi in a dream not to return to Herod. Obediently, they departed for their country by another route, protecting the child from danger. They returned home changed, not only by the miles they had traveled, but by the King they had met.

- Prayer: Lord, help me seek You above all things, like the wise men did.
- Reflecting Question: What distractions keep you from seeking Jesus fully?
- Key Verse: "They bowed down and worshiped him." (Matthew 2:11)
- Faith in Action: Set aside one thing this week to spend more time with God.
- Gratitude Prompt: Thank God for guiding you to Jesus.

The Boy with Five Loaves and Two Fish

The sun was high as Jesus and His disciples crossed the Sea of Galilee. When they reached the other side, crowds were already waiting. Word had spread about the miracles Jesus performed, and thousands came from nearby towns to see Him. Families gathered on the hillsides, eager to hear His teaching. Children ran ahead of their parents, and people carried baskets and blankets, ready to stay all day.

Jesus looked at the crowd and saw that they were hungry. More than five thousand men were there, not counting women and children. Turning to Philip, one of His disciples, He asked, "Where shall we buy bread for these people to eat?" Philip's eyes widened. "It would take more than half a year's wages to buy enough bread for each one to have a bite."

Andrew, another disciple, spoke up. "Here is a boy with five small barley loaves and two small fish, but how far will they go among so many?" The boy had been listening quietly, clutching the simple lunch his mother had packed for him. He stepped forward, willing to give what little he had. It was not much, just bread and fish, but it was everything he could offer.

Jesus smiled and told the people to sit down on the grass. He took the loaves from the boy's hands, lifted His eyes toward heaven, and gave thanks. Then He broke the bread and began handing it to the disciples. They, in turn, passed it out to the people sitting in rows across the hillside.

Something incredible happened. The bread and fish did not run out. Each time the disciples reached into their baskets, there was more to give. The food multiplied, filling the hands of mothers, fathers, children, and elders alike. The crowd ate until everyone was satisfied. Laughter and joy spread across the hillside as people shared the meal, amazed at what was happening before their eyes.

When the meal was finished, Jesus told His disciples to gather the leftovers so that nothing would be wasted. They collected twelve baskets full of pieces from the five small loaves left over by those who had eaten. The crowd whispered to one another in awe, saying, "Surely this is the Prophet who is to come into the world."

The boy watched as thousands of people were fed from the small gift he had offered. He had given what little he had, and in the hands of Jesus it had become more than enough.

- Prayer: Lord, use even the small things I offer for Your glory.
- Reflecting Question: What small gift can you offer to God today?
- Key Verse: "Here is a boy with five small barley loaves and two small fish." (John 6:9)
- Faith in Action: Share one small thing you have with someone in need.
- Gratitude Prompt: Thank God for multiplying your small efforts.

Jesus Raises Lazarus

In the small town of Bethany lived two sisters, Mary and Martha, and their brother Lazarus. They were close friends of Jesus, and He often visited their home. One day Lazarus became very sick. The sisters sent word to Jesus, saying, "Lord, the one you love is sick." They believed that if Jesus came quickly, He could heal their brother.

But when Jesus heard the news, He did not leave right away. Instead, He stayed where He was for two more days. He told His disciples, "This sickness will not end in death. It is for God's glory so that the Son of God may be glorified through it."

By the time Jesus finally arrived in Bethany, Lazarus had already been in the tomb for four days. The house was filled with mourners, and grief hung in the air. When Martha heard Jesus was near, she ran out to meet Him. Through tears she said, "Lord, if You had been here, my brother would not have died. But I know that even now God will give You whatever You ask."

Jesus answered her, "Your brother will rise again." Martha thought He was speaking of the final resurrection, but Jesus looked at her and declared, "I am the resurrection and the life. The one who believes in Me will live, even though they die."

Mary soon came to Jesus as well. Overcome with sorrow, she fell at His feet and repeated her sister's words: "Lord, if You had been here, my brother would not have died." When Jesus saw her weeping, His spirit was deeply moved. He asked to be taken to the tomb, and there, Jesus Himself wept.

Standing before the cave where Lazarus lay, Jesus commanded that the stone be rolled away. Martha hesitated, reminding Him that the body had been there four days. But Jesus said, "Did I not tell you that if you believe, you will see the glory of God?" The stone was moved, and Jesus prayed to the Father. Then He cried out in a loud voice, "Lazarus, come out!" To everyone's astonishment, the dead man walked out of the tomb, still wrapped in burial cloths. Jesus told them, "Take off the grave clothes and let him go." In that moment, life triumphed over death, and many who witnessed it put their faith in Him.

- Prayer: Lord, thank You that You bring life where there is death and hope where there is despair.
- Reflecting Question: How does Jesus' power over death give you confidence in your faith?
- Key Verse: "I am the resurrection and the life. The one who believes in me will live, even though they die." (John 11:25)
- Faith in Action: Comfort someone who is grieving this week with words of hope.
- Gratitude Prompt: Thank God for the gift of eternal life and write down one reason you are thankful for it today.

The Road to Damascus

Saul was a man feared by the early church. He was determined to destroy the followers of Jesus, dragging men and women out of their homes and throwing them into prison. With fire in his heart, he went to the high priest and asked for letters that would allow him to arrest any believers he found in Damascus.

As Saul traveled the road with his companions, the sun beat down on the desert path. Suddenly, a light from heaven flashed around him, brighter than anything he had ever seen. The brilliance knocked him to the ground. From within the light came a voice that shook the air.

"Saul, Saul, why are you persecuting me?"

Terrified, Saul asked, "Who are you, Lord?"

The answer came with power. "I am Jesus, whom you are persecuting. Now get up and go into the city, and you will be told what you must do."

When Saul opened his eyes, everything was dark. He could no longer see. His companions led him by the hand into Damascus. For three days he remained blind. He did not eat or drink, but waited in silence. In the city lived a disciple named Ananias. The Lord spoke to him in a vision, telling him to go and lay hands on Saul so he would regain his sight. Ananias hesitated. "Lord, I have heard many reports about this man and all the harm he has done to Your holy people."

But the Lord said, "Go. This man is my chosen instrument to proclaim my name to the nations."

With trembling faith, Ananias obeyed. He found Saul and placed his hands on him. "Brother Saul," he said, "the Lord Jesus, who appeared to you on the road, has sent me so that you may see again and be filled with the Holy Spirit."

Immediately, something like scales fell from Saul's eyes, and he could see once more. He rose, was baptized, and began to eat and regain his strength. The persecutor had become a follower. Saul's life was forever changed, and soon he would be known as Paul, the apostle who carried the gospel across the world.

- Prayer: Lord, transform my heart and use me for Your purpose.
- Reflecting Question: What area of your life do you want God to transform?
- Key Verse: "I am Jesus, whom you are persecuting." (Acts 9:5)
- Faith in Action: Share your personal story of faith with someone this week.
- Gratitude Prompt: Thank God for changing lives, including yours.

The New Heaven and New Earth

John was exiled on the island of Patmos, far from the people he once taught and encouraged. In the stillness of his isolation, God gave him a vision unlike anything he had ever seen. The heavens opened, and John was carried into a glimpse of the future that filled his heart with hope.

He saw a new heaven and a new earth. The old world with its pain, sorrow, and sin had passed away. The sea was gone, and with it every symbol of separation and fear. In its place stood the holy city, the New Jerusalem, descending from heaven like a radiant bride prepared for her husband. Its walls sparkled with precious stones, and its streets gleamed like pure gold.

John heard a loud voice from the throne declaring, "Look, God's dwelling place is now among the people, and he will live with them." No longer would there be distance between God and His people. He would be their God, and they would be His children forever.

As John watched, he saw that in this new world, sorrow and suffering were no more. God Himself would wipe away every tear from every eye. Death would be gone, as well as mourning, crying, and pain. Everything that once brought grief would vanish in the presence of the Lord who makes all things new.

The city was filled with light, not from the sun or moon, but from the glory of God and the Lamb. Gates stood open in every direction, welcoming nations from all corners of the earth. Flowing from the throne of God was the river of life, clear as crystal, bringing refreshment and healing. On each side of the river grew the tree of life, bearing fruit in every season, its leaves bringing healing to the nations.

Nothing impure would ever enter the city. The curse of sin would be gone forever. God's servants would see His face and serve Him with joy. There would be no night, no darkness, only the eternal light of God's presence.

As John gazed upon this vision, he knew it was not only a promise for someday. It was a certain future secured by Jesus, the Lamb who was slain yet lives forever. The new heaven and new earth stood as the final victory, the eternal home prepared for all who belong to Him.

- Prayer: Lord, thank You for the promise of eternal life in Your presence.
- Reflecting Question: How does the hope of eternity change the way you live today?
- Key Verse: "He will wipe every tear from their eyes." (Revelation 21:4)
- Faith in Action: Encourage someone with the hope of heaven this week.
- Gratitude Prompt: Write down 3 reasons you are thankful for eternal life.

Share Your Experience

Dear reader,

Thank you for spending time with this book. I hope that the stories you have read have encouraged your faith and reminded you of God's presence in your daily life. Writing and sharing these pages has been a journey of prayer and reflection, and my greatest hope is that they have been meaningful to you in some way.

Now I have a small request. Would you take just a moment to share your honest thoughts about this book in a review on Amazon? Your feedback, whether positive or constructive, matters deeply. It not only helps me grow as an author but also guides other readers who are searching for the kind of encouragement and insight you have just experienced.

Reviews are like light posts for those still deciding what to read. By leaving yours, you may help someone you will never meet discover the message they need at just the right time.

Scan to leave a review

Thank you for being part of this journey. I look forward to reading your words.

With gratitude,

Tobias.

www.ingramcontent.com/pod-product-compliance
Lightning Source LLC
LaVergne TN
LVHW081517060526
838200LV00005B/204